Noble Knights

A d20 Guide to Knightly Orders

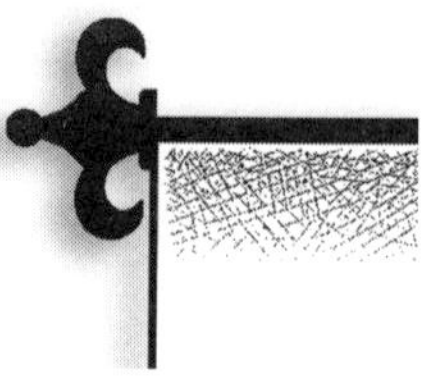

Avalanche Press Ltd.

P.O. Box 4775, Virginia Beach, VA 23454 USA

1-800-564-9008 • www.AvalanchePress.com

ISBN 1-932091-07-6

Printed in the United States of America. First Printing, 2003.

Table of Contents

Introduction 04

Chapter 1: A Brief History of Knighthood 05

- The Knight 05
- Squires 06
- The Making of a Knight 06
- Female Knights in the Middle Ages 07
- The Order of the Hatchet 07
- Other Orders of Knighthood 08
- Honor 08
- Heavy Cavalry 09
- Feudalism 09

Chapter 2: The Knights Templar 10

Chapter 3: The Knights of St. John of the Hospital 18

Chapter 4: The Knights of Santiago 29

Chapter 5: The Knights of St. James of Compostela 34

Chapter 6: The Knights of Calatrava 39

Chapter 7: The Order of the Knights of Christ 44

Chapter 8: The Teutonic Knights 47

Chapter 9: The Knights of the Garter 53

Chapter 10: The Order of St. Michael 57

Chapter 11: The Knights of the Holy Sepulchre 60

Chapter 12: Minor Orders 65

- Order of the Tower and the Sword 65
- Order of Avis 66
- Order of the Holy Ghost 67
- Order of the Dragon 68
- Order of the Swan 69
- Order of Bath 69
- Order of the Golden Fleece 71

Chapter 13: Creating Your Own Order 74

- Historical Period 74
- Primary Location 75
- Purpose 76
- Soldiers 76
- Hospitallers 76
- Advisors 76
- Oaths 76
- How Do I Join? 77
- Mechanics 77

Credits 78

Introduction

Knights are larger-than-life figures of romanticism and steel that spark the imagination and encourage dreams. The image of the heroic knight-in-shining-armor is a powerful one with its roots in chivalric tales and the legends of King Arthur. They are archetypes – portrayals of a desire for innocence and strength – but in reality, they were so much more.

Knighthood emerged during the Middle Ages when the Crusades against the Holy Land were in full swing and the world was overwhelmed with religious fervor and dedication. Religious devotion is at the heart of knighthood, and each of the knightly orders covered in this book reflects an example of at least one aspect of those principles. In this text, we look at the oldest knightly orders, their goals and dreams, their fanaticism and contrast them with Renaissance and later orders – where the fire of religion burned far less brightly, and knights were created as advisors and not as soldiers on the field.

Throughout history, knighthood has been seen as an emblem towards which to aspire; it is a sign that the individual has achieved a state beyond that of normal people. Their honor, chivalry, and prowess are respected simply because of their titles, and they are considered blessed by God for their state. Achieving that grace requires adventure, dedication, and luck. The role of knights in peace and war is clearly outlined, and each man (or, in rare cases, women) who wishes to bear the burden of knighthood must live up to those expectations.

The knightly orders in this book are each historically based, detailed while they were at their primes and reflecting their greatest achievements. Playing such a knight is a challenge – they are far more than sword-wielding, armor-wearing warriors. On or off the battlefield, knights were expected to live up to a code of conduct that could be far more stringent than that of a priest or a monk. Their duties are outlined, as well as the requirements for induction into the order so that new characters can seek the path of the knight. Through trial and adventure, they may join one of these august brotherhoods and find their place.

The body of this book covers ten separate and unique Knightly Orders suitable for inclusion in any historical or fantasy game world. They are covered in detail, including an overview, a history section, their ultimate goals and purposes, and information about how to join them. Note that these entries are historically accurate. While you might wish to include them in your fantasy campaign, you may need to make some adjustments depending on the tenor of the game you run. Many of the knightly orders described herein were dedicated to the slaughter of the Muslims, and they did so with relish. What may appear evil in the 21st Century, where we like to pretend that religious tolerance is the norm, seemed perfectly reasonable 800 years ago. Islamic peoples were all seen as a deadly threat that needed to be eliminated with the same speed and tenacity that many modern adventuring parties employ against marauding orcs. In fact, the orcish invaders of 21st-Century fantasy games have their roots in the Christian fear of Islamic expansion hundreds of years ago. It is important to bear this in mind when reading about the exploits of the Knights Templar or the Knights of Calatrava.

Near the end of this work, you'll find a section designed to give you information and ideas on creating and fleshing out your own knightly orders. Why do they exist, what are their purposes, where could they be based – these questions are all covered to give you ideas and information to work with on your own. Every campaign is different, and the details and attention given to a knightly order can make it extremely memorable and fun to play.

So mount your destrier and take up your lance. There is a threat to the king that only the boldest of Noble Knights can repel. This book is your gateway to adventure in service to the Crown and the Church.

Chapter 1: A Brief History of Knighthood

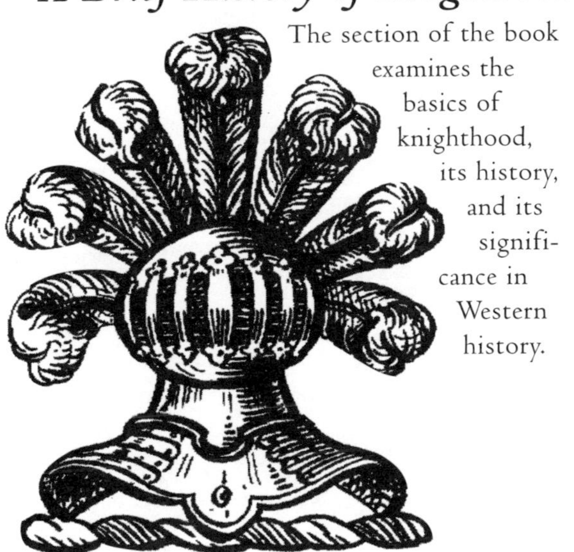

The section of the book examines the basics of knighthood, its history, and its significance in Western history.

The Knight

Our images of chivalry and knighthood are of men in sterling armor, jousting on a tournament field or saving damsels from high towers. Knights wear emblazoned surcoats with red crosses, ride massive steeds with iron hooves, and live a life of nobility and gentility. These are stereotypes fostered by the age of courtly love, by those who remained at home during the Crusades and who created tales of honor and chivalry to pass the dark nights in front of the fire. Knights, truly, are much more – and much less – than their legend.

The word descends from the French word for "horseman" – *chevalier.* The term denoted a man of great standing and noble lineage, someone who is capable of equipping himself with a warhorse and following in the footsteps of his king. Their oaths, sworn upon the badge of their nobility and on the blade of their weapon, call them into noble service in all parts of the world. Chivalry is more than a birthright: it is an order, a chosen path that must be achieved and granted by an authority figure that inducts each member according to worth.

Chivalry cannot be divorced from the martial world, nor can its warlike implications be ignored. It is not an order of tailors or courtiers but a sovereign corps of fighting men ready and willing to give their lives for their faith. Their duty was to defend the medieval Church, its clergy, and the faithful parishioners from the evils of the Muslim world. Because of these duties, chivalry became transformed from a secular and militant order into a religious one – still asked to fight and defend but on a basis of faith rather than by the command of kings.

Several poems, texts, and manuscripts were written about knighthood and chivalry, ranging from the historic documents of the Holy Land and the Crusades to the flowery poetry of England and France, glorifying war and battle. One of the most important and revealing works is the *Libre del Ordre de Cavayleria* written by Ramon Lull in the 1300's. The book opens with an account of chivalry's origins (both real and imagined). According to this work, when evil entered the world after the Fall, the virtue of chivalry was added to the world by God's own hand in order to restrain and defend the people. One man in every thousand was chosen by God to hold forth this banner. Those individuals were chosen because they were the "most loyal, most strong, and of most noble courage." The horse, "most noble of beasts" was given to this man in order to aid him in his fight, and the other men were tasked to create food and weapons so that the knight could defend them with his battle-prowess.

It was further the duty of every knight to train his first son in the ways of chivalry so that the practice would not die out. This included training in horsemanship, battle, and courtesy as well as the normal education received by a child of noble birth. Chivalry was respected and idolized, and even the lesser sons of kings dedicated their lives to knighthood, both out of faith in the knighthood's purposes and because of the position of prominence within the Church and the State that was granted by joining such an order.

In the 11th and 12th Centuries, the Crusades in the Middle East called forth enormous armies from all over Europe in order to invade and "reclaim" the Holy Land. These men found themselves released from the constraints of feudalism, and they bonded together in organizations called "knightly orders," designed to be both military and religious orders of chivalry. The earliest of these orders were fraternities of like-minded men gathered to serve a particular purpose – the Templars swore to defend Jerusalem, while the Hospitallers vowed to serve the poor, sick, and wounded. All of the knights of these orders were men of noble birth, drawn from a particular social class and bound together in a common purpose.

Squires

Every knight was required to have a squire to serve him, a young man learning the tenets and code of the knight. These squires might be the knight's own first-born son or the sons of other nobles, fostered out to serve the knight and earn their place in society. Every squire was expected to follow certain codes of honor, and achieve excellence in the service of his master. According to the *Libre del Ordre de Cavayleria,* the squire must be "able-bodied, and of sufficient age to discharge the tasks of manhood. He should come of good lineage and must have sufficient wealth to support his rank. He must have valor and nobility, and be without reproach. The candidate for knighthood must be a Christian, brave, true to his promise, faithful to the Church and his lord, and zealous in defense of the weak, especially of women and orphans." When the squire had satisfied his knight's tests and served not less than five years, he was eligible for knighthood.

At Pentecost, Christmas, and Easter, squires who proved their worth were taken to one of the great cathedrals - Notre Dame, St. Stefan, etc. - and asked to stand vigil. Knighthood might be conferred on the field of battle, but more often it was given during one of the great Church festivals and was a far more ceremonial affair. For 24 hours, the squire knelt before the altar and prayed to God for cleansing. He confessed his sins before a priest and then spent the night in prayer and contemplation "beneath the eyes of God." These would be his last actions as a squire and his first as a knight.

The Making of a Knight

When a noble squire came of age and it was time for him to become a knight, the one he served (along with others of his order) would gather in a sacred site on a holy day and perform a grand but solemn religious ceremony. During the entirety of the night before, the young squire was left alone praying and meditating in church, kneeling before the altar on which lay his sword, his shield, and his lance.

The next morning came a bath, traditionally in a stream or a large tub of icy water. The water was not heated because the squire was expected to prove himself strong and hardy, able to accept hardships in the name of his knighthood and in the face of God. Raised from the bath by priests, the squire was then clad in fresh new garments, which were almost always white. These clothes symbolized the squire's soul, pure and reborn through his faith in God and his holy vigil. They were a symbol of purity and faith, blessed by the priests and hand-woven by either the squire's mother or the nuns of the monastery. Over this white tunic was placed a

red robe, symbolic of the blood he would be called upon to shed in defense of the oppressed; and over this a black garment, representing the mystery of death.

The squire was then led away from the altar by the priests. He attended Mass, knelt before an assemblage of knights of the order he wished to join, and listened to a sermon about his new life and duties. His sword (usually given by his father or by the knight the young man served as a squire) was laid upon the altar and blessed in the name of God and the order. His armor might be standing by as well, waiting to be blessed by the attending priests in the hopes that God would lend it strength to protect this faithful servant of the Church. Because a knight was expected to be a lover of Christ and a defender of the Church, his weapons had to be consecrated to God's cause.

After the sermon and consecrations, the young man was brought forward to kneel before the altar and the assembled priests. In full view of his order and God, he made solemn vows to defend the Church, be true to the king, and help women in distress. He swore to dedicate his life to right, justice, and holy sanctity. The three most sacred oaths: those of poverty, humility, and chastity, were administered by the high priest, and the young man would then take communion.

At this point in the service, the knight with the highest rank in the assemblage came forward to confer upon the young man his order of knighthood. Typically, the highest-ranking knight was flanked by the knight whose squire was being raised, and, if a different person, by the squire's father or family priest. The young man knelt before these knights with clasped hands, and solemnly vowed before all to uphold religion, chivalry, and honor.

The knightly lord then buckled the youth's sword on to the young man's side while the priests placed upon his heels the golden spurs of knighthood. His armor was presented to him, and he would be girded in it, and then the squire would kneel one final time. At this point, the highest-ranking knight would draw his own weapon and place the blade upon the young man's right shoulder. Tapping him lightly on the shoulders with his sword, the lord pronounced over him the solemn words: "In the name of God, of St. Michael, and of St. George, I dub thee knight. Be valiant, fearless, and loyal." When the young man rose, he was considered truly and fully a knight.

Another ceremony of knighthood included an unusual practice – the "last blow." According to tradition, knights were expected to return blow for blow any insult dealt them, their rank, or the Church. At the end of the knighting ceremony, therefore, the priest would step forward and give him a blow with the palm of the hand, adding the words "Be a valiant knight!" This blow would go unanswered, and was to be the last unanswered blow that the knight would ever receive.

Female Knights in the Middle Ages

There were two ways anyone could be a knight: by holding land under a knight's fee or by being made a knight or inducted into an order of knighthood. There are examples of both cases for women.

The Order of the Hatchet

There was a clearly military order of knighthood for women. It was the Order of the Hatchet *(orden de la Hacha)* in Catalonia. It was founded in 1149 by Raymond Berenger, Count of Barcelona, to honor the women who fought for the defense of the town of Tortosa against a Moorish attack. The dames admitted to the order received many privileges, including exemption from all taxes, and took precedence over men in public assemblies. The order appears to have died out with the original members.

Historian Josef Micheli Marquez refers to the Noble Women of Tortosa in Aragon as *Cavalleros* or "knights." Don Raymond, last Earl of Barcelona gained the city of Tortosa from the Moors but nearly lost it once more. In 1150, the Moors laid siege to it again. The inhabitants were nearly overcome, and, in desperation, they turned to their own people for defense. The Earl could not send troops, and, because the peasants of Tortosa were ill-trained and equipped, the men decided that their only course was to surrender. However, the women, hearing that their men were going to surrender and leave them and their children to the mercy of the Moors, put on men's clothes and, with an amazing and resolute attack against the Moors, managed to break the siege and free the city.

The Earl was impressed and astonished by the gallantry and bravery of the action and therefore instituted an order of knighthood into which were admitted only those brave women who fought for the city of Tortosa. He assigned to them a badge, the right to bear arms, and all the honors and privileges of knighthood. Their badge was that of a red cross, sharp at the top and resembling a torch of crimson. It was to be worn upon their bodices or bonnets to show that they were honored members of the court of Aragon. He also ordained that at all meetings of the city of Tortega, the women should have precedence over the men in all things and should be allowed an equal or greater vote in the city's proceedings. These women were further exempted from all taxes and granted a royal stipend (much like the tribute and duty given to a knight) by the Crown.

Other Orders of Knighthood

Medieval French possesses two words, *chevaleresse* and *chevalière,* which were used in two ways: one was for the wife of a knight, and this usage goes back to the 14th Century. The other designated a female knight with her own order of chivalry and induction.

Several established military orders associated with women in many ways, beyond the simple provision of nuns to aid in the hospices. The Teutonic Order accepted *consorores* who assumed the habit of the order and lived under its rule; they undertook menial and hospitaller functions. In Italy, the Order of the Glorious Saint Mary, founded by Loderigo d'Andalo, a nobleman of Bologna, in 1233 and approved by Pope Alexander IV in 1261, was the first religious order of knighthood to grant the rank of *militissa* to women. This order was suppressed by Sixtus V in 1558.

In the Low Countries, at the initiative of Catherine Baw in 1441 and 10 years later of Elizabeth, Mary, and Isabella of the House of Hornes, orders were founded which were open exclusively to women of noble birth, who received the French title of *chevalière* or the Latin title of *equitissa.*

Ladies were appointed to the English Order of the Garter almost from the start. In all, 68 ladies were inducted between 1358 and 1488, including all consorts. Though many were women of royal blood or wives of Knights of the Garter, some women were neither. They wore the garter on the left arm, and some are shown on their tombstones with this arrangement.

In England, Buckland was the site of a house of Hospitaller sisters from Henry II's reign to 1540. In Aragon, there were Hospitaller convents in Sigena, San Salvador de Isot, Grisén, Alguaire, headed each by a commendatrix. In France, they are found in Beaulieu (near Cahors), Martel, and Fieux. The only other military order to have convents by 1300 was the Order of Santiago, which admitted married members since its foundation in 1175.

Honor

For a medieval knight, the ideal of "honor" meant far more than those of courage or skill. The honor of a knight was linked to his faith in God; to fail in one meant that the knight was flawed in the other. Knights would go to great lengths to prove their honor or to defend it against all insults. The concept of chivalry developed from a warrior's code into a sophisticated system of morals, faith, and values to which all knights were supposed to adhere.

The duties of a knight extended on and off the battlefield, covering every aspect of their lives. Their code insisted on personal integrity, their duty to defend the weak from oppression, and the practice of knightly virtues. Those virtues included *largesse,* the virtue of generosity toward those less fortunate; *pite,* the virtue of compassion and mercy; *franchise,* or frankness and the ability to tell the truth and keep a noble and free spirit; and *courtoisie,* the virtue of courtliness and noble behavior, particularly toward women and toward one's superiors in the state and the Church.

The more traditional virtues of a warrior were also mentioned, but these fell behind the more noble virtues listed above. A knight must also be bold and brave, fearless in the defense of his church and his people and able to tell justice from iniquity and act accordingly. His abilities on the field of battle were repeatedly tested but seen as secondary to the purity of the soul.

But this chivalrous ideal came from the second half of the Middle Ages, propagated by those who did not have to see the massacres and insanity of the Crusades upon the Holy Land. Those knights who were versed in the true dangers and "glories" of war often had a different version of the Knightly Code – one which left no room for mercy or compassion in the face of battle.

Wealthy knights might double or triple this entourage. The romantic image of a lone knight errant is strictly a literary invention. A lone knight was generally a miserable figure, down on his luck, and extraordinarily vulnerable.

Heavy Cavalry

The original battle-ready knight was little more than another formation of heavy cavalry. Charlemagne is credited with the development of these warriors, known as elite lancers.

This secular "knight" was the central figure of a tactical and logistic unit based around his heavy horse and armor. The footmen were designed to sweep away lesser resistance while the knight drove heavy force into the body of the opposing army, crushing its resistance and placing himself in the midst of foes. A basic Lance was comprised as follows: A heavily armed knight with a destrier (warhorse), riding into the fray with arms bared and behind a heavy shield of plate mail and steel. With him rode a lightly armed squire to care for the horse and equipment, typically riding a mule or light horse. Behind this pair marched five to 10 heavy footmen, whose job it was to finish off anyone unhorsed by the knight. Those heavily-armored individuals who fell on the field would be unable to rise again in time to defend themselves against the shorter weapons of the marching infantry.

Feudalism

The values and organization of feudal society were incredibly vital to the foundation and continuance of knightly orders. The feudal system of the Middle Ages allowed for knights to fit within the social order while still receiving their commands from a source of faith – the Catholic Church. Their duties and obligations bridged the gap between the secular and spiritual, allowing for both sides of moral leadership to find a harmony within the actions and unity of the knightly orders.

Feudalism was a reliant social structure, wherein each strata of the nation was dependant on the one below it and above it. These tight, caste-like systems allowed each rank of society to know their duties and obligations clearly. At the lowest rank were the serfs, the indentured servants, and those who owned no possessions. Above them were the peasants, who farmed the land and took care of the beasts. At the next level were the middle-class, the laborers and artists, and those who manufactured goods and used their talents to construct items from raw materials. Above these were the merchants, the wealthiest of the middle classes, and above them (in rank, at least, if not in noble bearing) were the lowest echelons of landed society. The low-ranking nobles, such as esquires, landed knights, and baronets were just beneath the lords, barons, counts and dukes. Above them were the true leaders and elite of society – the kings, emperors, and highest nobles of the land.

The knightly orders fit into this system in an unusual manner. Both secular and spiritual, they paid no taxes to their nations and owed their fealty only to the Church and to their respective kings. Effectively, they were a chain of feudalism all to themselves and did not fit in any of the usual strata of society. Their fiefs were considered Church property, and their monasteries could hoard all the money they gathered from tribute without sharing anything or paying taxes. While this led to very prosperous orders, it was also the downfall of the knightly class in the long run as impoverished princes and greedy kings destroyed the knights in order to seize their money and their support.

Chapter 2: The Knights Templar

The Knights Templar are the earliest founders of the military orders, and are the type on which the others are modeled. They are marked in history by their humble beginning, by their marvelous growth, and by their tragic end. Originally, the Knights Templar were members of a religious military order of Crusaders in Jerusalem. Also known as the Order of the Poor Knights of the Temple of Solomon, they wore a white tabard with a red cross on the front in order to distinguish themselves from other Knightly orders. The seal of the Knights Templar was the sigil of two knights on one horse, showing their poverty and humility.

The Knights Templar were founded to protect temples and pilgrims along the path from Europe to the Holy Lands They took a vow of poverty, which was rare for knights, who had to supply themselves with a horse, armor, and weapons. As was common with temple guardians, the Knights Templar were not allowed any association with women. Their faith and loyalty were unquestioned, proven on the battlefield and within the Church. Many of the ancient relics of Jerusalem were given into their care, including, some believe, the legendary Shroud of Turin, in the folds of which Jesus was buried.

Because the Knights Templar regularly transmitted money and supplies from Europe to Palestine, they gradually developed an efficient banking system unlike any the world had seen before. Their military might and financial acumen caused them to become both feared and trusted. Because of their unselfish defense of the Holy Lands and their monastic vows, they amassed great wealth through gifts from their grateful benefactors. They soon had an army and a fleet as well as surplus money that they used to fund other major Christian projects. Since the Knights had taken a vow of poverty, they re-invested the money and became the most powerful order of money-lenders in Christendom. So great was their influence that they could demand receipt of all monies loaned to a country and completely bankrupt that nation's economy. Because of this incredible leverage, the "Poor Order of Knights" was in fact one of the most powerful organizations in the Middle Ages.

Their castles were both monasteries and cavalry-barracks and showed clearly that the life of a Templar Knight was full of contrasts – both rich and bound by oaths of poverty; sworn to serve yet commanding armies and pulling myriad political strings. A contemporary describes the Templars as "both lions of war and lambs at the hearth; rough knights on the battlefield, pious monks in the chapel; formidable to the enemies of Christ, gentleness itself towards His friends." Having renounced all the pleasures of life, they faced death with a proud indifference. It was well known that the Knights Templar would never surrender on the field of honor: they were the first to attack, the last to retreat, obedient and yet fierce upon the field. The Templars fought alongside Richard, the Lion Hearted and other crusaders in the battles for the Holy Lands, and their deeds resonated throughout the Middle Ages.

As an army, the Knights Templar were never very numerous, but their numbers contained fanatic warriors and loyal servants of Christianity who would gladly martyr themselves. The Knights Templar did not care about a man's past when they accepted him as brother so long as he passed their tests and proved his loyalty. Even excommunicated men who wished to expiate their sins were admitted gladly into the order. All that was required of a new member was a blind obedience, as imperative in the soldier as in the monk. To prove his sincerity, he was subjected to a secret test to prove his faith and loyalty. Faith and fraternity counted for more than past deeds, and many wealthy sons were turned away when it was determined that they did not have the heart and spirit to serve the order loyally.

When Templars were defeated, they would die in prison since their order was forbidden to offer a ransom for their brothers-in-arms. When taken prisoner by Muslims, they scornfully refused the freedom offered them on condition of conversion and always remained loyal to the Christian faith. At the siege of Safed in 1264, at which 90 Templars met death, 80 others were taken prisoner, and, refusing to deny Christ, died martyrs to the Faith.

History

Immediately after the deliverance of Jerusalem, the Crusaders, considering their vow fulfilled, returned in a body to

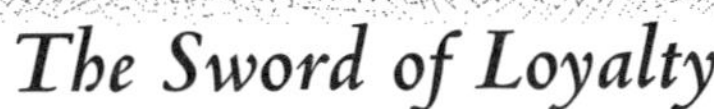

The Sword of Loyalty

The Sword of Loyalty is a +3 Holy longsword, and conforms to the following stats:

Damage: 1d8 (Subdual Damage only) (plus Holy Damage of 2d6, also Subdual)

Crit: 19-20 x2

Range: —

Weight: 3 lb

Type: Slashing

The Sword of Loyalty bestows one Negative Level on any evil creature that attempts to wield it. The Negative Level remains as long as the creature holds the weapon and disappears when it is released.

All damage dealt by the Sword of Loyalty is Subdual; it cannot be used to deal Lethal Damage and will not retain an edge to its blade. Each time a target is dealt Subdual damage by this weapon, it must make a Will Save against a DC equal to the total number of points of Subdual Damage dealt by the Sword of Loyalty. Targets failing this Saving Throw have their Alignment changed to Lawful Good for 10 minutes per Level of the wielder, and, if the wielder is Good-aligned, the target will view him or her as a trusted ally. If the target takes all of its Hit Points in subdual damage, its alignment immediately and permanently becomes Lawful Good (such alignment changes can only be reversed through a great deal of role-play and time).

The Sword of Loyalty can never be used against Lawful Good creatures or against faithful members of the Knights Templar (whatever their alignment may be). In these instances, the sword simply does no damage, no matter how brutally wielded.

their homes. The defense of this precarious conquest, surrounded as it was by Mohammedan neighbors, remained. In 1118, a knight named Hugues de Payens and eight companions bound themselves by a perpetual vow, taken in the presence of the Patriarch of Jerusalem, to defend the newly founded Christian kingdom. The King accepted their services and assigned them a portion of his palace, adjoining the temple of the city for their living quarters (because they had none); and as a moniker to distinguish this new order of knights, they were termed the "Poor Knights of the Temple."

Hugues de Payens journeyed to the West to seek the approbation of the Church for his newly founded monastic order and to obtain recruits to increase the safety of Jerusalem. At the Council of Troyes (1128), the Knights Templar knelt before the pope and were officially created as an Order of the Church. They accepted not only the three perpetual vows of chastity, poverty, and obedience but also the crusader's vow, and many other austere rules to govern their existence as an order.

The Knights Templar began to develop their own sigils, symbols, and attire. They adopted the white habit of the Cistercians, adding to it a red cross to symbolize their task to defend Jerusalem. Although the order was poor and austere, recruits flocked to the new order and swelled its ranks with the faithful warriors of Christianity. Originally, the Knights Templar were comprised of four ranks of brethren. These were the knights, equipped like the heavy cavalry of the Middle Ages; the sergeants, who formed the light cavalry; and two ranks of non-fighting men: farmers entrusted with the administration of temporal material; and chaplains, who were expected to minister to the spiritual needs of the order.

The order owed its rapid growth in popularity to the fact that it combined the two great passions of the Middle Ages: religious fervor and martial prowess. Even before the Templars proved their worth, the ecclesiastical and lay authorities offered favors and accolades to them for their choice of duty and their loyalty to Jerusalem and to the Church. The pope took the Knights Templar under his immediate protection, exempting them from all other jurisdiction whether Episcopal or secular. Their property was assimilated to the Church estates and exempted from all taxation, even from the ecclesiastical tithes. In every way, they were supported and encouraged to grow as an order.

However, their good fortune brought conflict as well as prosperity. As their landed property grew and the order obtained barracks, keeps, and castles, their exemption from tithes became a thorn in the side of many kings and other nobles. Despite their vow of poverty, the Templars owned a great deal of land. They owned territory in every state, country, and major province of Europe. In France, they formed more than 11 bailiwicks, subdivided into more than 42 commanderies; the Knights Templar of Spain possessed much the same; even in distant Palestine their presence was still notable. A contemporary tells us that there were 400 Knights Templar in the city of Jerusalem at the zenith of their prosperity.

The Templars were opposed by the Order of Hospitallers, which was another knightly sect. Due to the infighting between the two groups and their inability to work together, Jerusalem was lost once more to the Muslims. The Templars sacrificed themselves with their customary bravery, but were, nevertheless, partly responsible for the downfall of Jerusalem.

Famous Castles

Many of the most famous Templar castles of the Holy Land are still standing. The remarkable ruins that remain include the keep of Safed, built in 1140; Karak, a castle in the deep desert built in 1143; and, most importantly of all, Castle Pilgrim, built in 1217 to command a strategic defile on the sea-coast.

To put an end to this baneful rivalry between the military orders, there was a very simple remedy at hand, namely their amalgamation. This was officially proposed by the French king Louis IX (Saint Louis) at the Council of Lyons in 1274. It was proposed anew in 1293 by Pope Nicholas IV. This idea was supported by the Christian populace, who demanded the existing orders wither, merge, or create a third order to replace them.

Despite the vow of poverty that all Knights Templar took, the order became wealthy very early after several prosperous crusades into Jerusalem, donations from affluent patrons, and excavations at the Temple in Jerusalem. Ironically, the Knights Templar grew even richer by giving away their money. They became bankers to Christendom, loaning their money to nations as well as powerful nobles, and soon their interests doubled and even tripled.

Meanwhile, the Christian Kings were preparing for war once more. Philip the Fair, the grandson of St. Louis, proposed a second Crusade to retake Jerusalem. Phillip envied the wealth of both orders of Knights and planned to seize their goods and moneys in order to fund his new crusade. Yet he still needed a pretext since seizing possessions that formed part of the ecclesiastical domain was sacrilege.

At last, he recruited the aid of a weak-willed pope (Clement IV), and seized upon a singular solution. The Templars were named heretics to the Church, their orthodoxy questioned and condemned, and Phillip seized their wealth for his own.

On the strength of these "new ecclesiastical revelations," orders were sent throughout France to arrest all the Knights Templar. On October 13, 1307, the body of the order was arrested and forced to submit to a rigorous examination of their faith and beliefs. Their imprisonment led to the deaths of thousands of Templars. Because there was very little evidence to support the claim that the Knights Templar were in fact heretics, Philip was forced to convict them only through their own confession. To extort such admissions, the use of torture was considered necessary and legitimate.

Money

With its accumulated revenues from property and other treasures, the Knights Templar amassed a great amount of wealth, which was deposited in its temples at Paris and London. After the Crusades were over, the knights returned to their chapters throughout Europe and became money lenders to monarchs, kingdoms, and principalities. In the process, they invented much of the modern banking system, including inflation, money-changing, and other capital gains. Numerous princes and private individuals banked with the Knights Templar owing to their forthrightness and solid credit. In Paris, the royal treasure was kept in the Temple of the Knights Templar.

Most of the accused subsequently declared themselves guilty of these secret crimes. Some made confessions without the use of torture but in fear of it. Even the Grand Master of the Knights Templar, Jacques de Molay, acknowledged later that he had lied and condemned his order so that he might save his own life.

As for the members, the Templars recognized as guiltless were allowed either to join another military order or to return to the secular state. In the latter case, a pension for life, charged to the possessions of the order, was granted them. On the other hand, the Templars who had pleaded guilty before their bishops were to be treated "according to the rigors of justice, tempered by a generous mercy."

The pope reserved to his own judgment the cause of the grand master and his three first dignitaries. They had confessed their guilt; it remained to reconcile them with the Church after they had testified to their repentance with

The Skull of Sidon

The Skull and Crossbones have long been known to have connections to the Knights Templar. It was commonly used as a symbol on Templar gravesites in the past. The Skull and Crossbones point out our own mortality and eventual death. This image was believed to figure in many of the secret Templar rituals. The legend of this symbol's origin is gruesome in the extreme.

The Knights Templar were monastic in nature and therefore forbidden to have intercourse with women. Legend states that one Templar knight in Sidon was in love with a woman who died. Mad with grief at his beloved's death, the knight dug up her corpse and physically consummated their relationship. After nine months, a voice from the void bade him return to her grave. The knight obeyed, and, at the appointed time he opened the coffin again and found that the dead woman had born him a son of sorts.

A tiny skull rested on the leg bones of the skeleton. The same voice bade the knight to "guard it well, for it would be the giver of all good things," and so the knight carried the child's skull as well as the woman's leg bones away with him. It became his protecting genius, and he was able to defeat his enemies by merely showing them the magic skull and crossbones. In due course, these relics passed into the possession of the order.

the customary solemnity. But at the supreme moment the grand master recovered his courage and proclaimed the innocence of the Templars and the falsity of his own alleged confessions. By order of Philip the Fair, Jacques de Molay and his immediate officers in the Knights Templar were burned at the stake before the gates of the palace. De Molay is said to have cursed King Philip and Pope Clement as he burned, asking both men to join him within a year. Clement died only one month later and Philip IV seven months after that.

The Holy Land

Jerusalem's history stretches back more than 5,000 years, into historical obscurity. It is known that a tribe of Canaanites inhabited the city first, and that they remained there for over a thousand years. Next, an invasion from Persia seized the city, holding it until 333 BC, when Palestine was brought into the empire of Alexander the Great. The Jews later revolted, defeating the invaders and liberating the city from the Syrians.

The Romans set up a local dynasty, led by the infamous House of Herod, to rule Palestine. This leadership took over Jerusalem with an iron hand, but Herod brought his own advancements to the city. Herod rebuilt much of Jerusalem, including the Temple, but his rulership was circumvented by Roman governors who retained ultimate control. The most famous governor, Pontius Pilate, authorized the execution of Jesus Christ.

In 135, after the failure of a massive revolt, Jews were banished from Jerusalem. From the early 4th Century, Jerusalem developed as a center of Christian pilgrimage, and thousands of religious tribes flocked into the city – including Jews, who often concealed their faith in order to live in the holy city. Except for a brief period of Persian rule, the city remained solidly under the control of the Roman government until 638.

Then, a massive religious upheaval in the Middle East ended with Muslim Arabs in control of Jerusalem. The Muslims built a new religious center – the Dome of the Rock mosque – on the site of a fallen Jewish Temple. In the 11th Century, Muslim toleration of both Jews and Christians gave way to persecution. Muslims destroyed both Christians and Jews, removing their presence from the city almost entirely. European Christendom responded by launching the Crusades, which conquered Jerusalem in 1099 and continued to cause war and disruption for several hundred years.

Organization

The purpose of the Order of Knights Templar was to defend and keep sacred the Holy Land, including but not limited to the city of Jerusalem, where their order was founded. They served God, the Church, and their own purposes – to control the governments of Europe and influence them to help defend and protect the Holy Land and keep the Church's interests safe.

Another purported desire of the Knights Templar was to keep safe the line of David. According to this legend, Christ – a descendent of King David – and Mary Magdalene had children. The Knights Templar were charged with tracing the lineage of this offspring and recording all births and deaths within it. Rumor further has it that they continue in this duty even today, long after their order was allegedly "destroyed."

They never had many knights, but the order also organized sergeants, farmers, and chaplains. They built or held numerous castles, and also churches, which they called temples, and which were usually round. But even they could not hold back the Islamic tide.

Ten to 20 Templars work together as a legion, calling their group a "banner." Ten to 20 such banners form a full squadron, made up of approximately 200 knights. Such a squadron is usually assigned to a single keep or small location, training together each day in order to sharpen their abilities. Five to 10 of these squadrons form a group known as a "battle," although it is exceptionally rare to see a full battle unit engaged. The Knights Templar rarely have the manpower to field such a unit, and their squadrons are typically spread out over several large countries or areas, unable to gather for war.

Battles, when they can be engaged, are generally arranged in five groups: the Van, Left and Right Wings, the Center or Main Battle, and the Rear Guard. The size, distribution and character of these forces vary according to the force against which they would be fighting. The battles are not trained

Armor of the Knights Templar

Type: Full Plate Armor

AC Bonus: +11 (+8 base, +3 enchantment)

Max Dex Bonus: +3

Armor Check Penalty: -3

Arcane Spell Failure: 25%

Speed: 20 ft

Weight: 30 lb

This magical suit of battle-armor was forged by the first Grand Master of the Knights Templar. It has since been worn by the Grand Master or, on rare occasion, by a Champion or other prestigious member of the order for formal occasion. It has seen Jerusalem, traveled to Avalon and Aragon, and defended the goals of the righteous for hundreds of years. The armor is considered one of the most sacred relics of the Knights Templar, and is protected and cared for with almost religious respect.

The armor is sterling silver in color, forged from the finest steel and inlaid with gold and red tracings across the shoulders and breastplate. The front plate is emblazoned with the red cross of the Knights Templar and shines with a brilliant red flame when the bearer of the armor fights against Muslims, Moors, or other enemies of the Catholic Church. The armor is exceptionally forged of very light plates and weighs much less than ordinary plate mail.

Shield of the Knights Templar

Type: Large Metal Shield

AC Bonus: +3 (+2 base, +1 enchantment)

Armor Check Penalty: 0

Arcane Spell Failure: 5%

Weight: 5 lb

This shield is painted with the formal badge of the Knights Templar and glows with a soft, faint light at all times as if it were constantly reflecting the sun. It provides the equivalent of a Light spell that cannot be turned off, and the shield provides an additional +2 Magical Bonus against creatures harmed by sunlight (vampires, etc.).

to fight together due to the Knights' widespread membership, and breaking down such a large unit into smaller, more easily controlled groups is a great benefit to the troop's stability. The lower groups are organized around feudal lords under hire by the Templars for their military ability.

The Templars employed the same basic structure used by the secular armies, but their orientation was far stricter. Templars were ruled by their superiors with an iron fist. Templars were very different from their secular counterparts because they fully expected the submission of their free will to their commander. They never questioned orders, nor did they turn away from strange or seemingly suicidal commands. Their loyalty was sterling, and the ability to follow was reinforced daily. This important characteristic was not present in secular medieval forces, which were primarily made up of wealthy nobles' sons and peasants. These secular knights were very independent, using their knightly title more to join court than to fight on the field. Some of them were not even trained well for battle, and were certainly not capable of mass fights. By contrast, Templars possessed a high degree of discipline and conformity. The concept of the monastic vow of obedience is that a monk should obey the instructions of his abbot as if he were obeying the Lord.

The detailed deployment of Templar forces during a campaign isn't a very adequately organized endeavor, and often the Templar forces were arranged in a semi-random method. The equipment and logistical support that the Templars received during battle was often random and chaotic and was brought by whichever cloisters happened to have armor or stores ready when they received the call to arms.

A Knight of the Order

The soldiers of the Knights Templar take vows of poverty, fidelity, and chastity, and they take those vows very seriously. A common knight wears no more ornate garb than a monk, and maintains only a simple steed and basic armor for the times when he is called upon to fight. Their robes are typically white or homespun brown, marked with the order's cross upon the chest. They are not individually wealthy like many members of other knightly orders, and they are very bound to their vow of poverty.

Knights Templar typically remain within their compounds, rarely leaving to explore the outside world unless the order is called upon to right some wrong or supply the holy and just with a fighting sword. In general, the common knight is moderately young (as the older knights are either advanced within the order or have found a martyred death on the battlefield) and well-trained with the sword.

Older Knights Templar have more elaborate garb, usually ceremonial, but also wear lowly monk's robes when they are retiring within their compound or keep. Their badges of station are usually a simple neck-chain, or cloak with the order's insignia upon it, and their steed and arms may be of better quality than a common member of the order.

The leaders of the Knights Templar possess far better garb since they must be seen in courtly situations. Their robes are woven of fine linen, but still bear the cross of the Knights Templar both on the front of the robe and on the sweeping cloak that is usually worn as accoutrement. Their neck-chains are of gold, and their swords are usually of the highest caliber. Such knights are treated with respect and deference both inside and outside the order's walls.

Arms of the Knights Templar

The seal and arms of the Knights Templar are known throughout Europe. Knights wear the red cross patee, a cross with four equal arms and wide ends, which is stitched to or dyed upon their white robes and cloaks. The order's seal, used on paper and items of great significance, is two knights riding the same horse. It was designed to illustrate the vow of poverty to which all knights adhere.

Their battle flag was called *le Beauseant* and depicted their arms in a very unique manner. Most versions of the Templar flag have four quarters done in checked black and white, with a red cross patee in the center. Other, later variants had the red cross in the flag with straight arms much like the St. George cross of England. *"Beauseant!"* is also the battle cry of the Knights Templar as they rode into battle – it means roughly, "Be glorious!"

How Do I Join?

Joining the Knights Templar requires an oath to the Church and to the Order promising to abide by the triple vows of chastity, poverty, and obedience. Further, it requires the petitioner to put aside all vestiges of his previous life and take a new name among the Knightly Order. Once done, he can never go back to his previous life except by a grant from the pope (delivered only in extreme circumstance).

After this, the initiate undergoes a rigorous five-year training course designed to teach weaponry, mathematics, and other higher learning. When it is complete, the initiate is considered a full brother of the order, with all the privileges of a knight. Only through years of dedicated service can that knight become a master of the order – and it is far more likely that the knight will reach a martyr's death on the battlefield than that he will live long enough and have the courtly savvy to become a master in the politics of the Knights Templar.

The House of the Templars

The Templars enlarged a magnificent Mosque in western Jerusalem, building their fortress within a sacred structure. In addition, they built partitions to divide the mosque's prayer hall into living quarters – cells appropriate to the habit and care of a monk or knight. The Templars even used the vaults supporting the Temple Mount structures as stables, as described by John of Wurtzburg:

When you descend to the main street, there is a great gate through which one may enter the great courtyard of the Temple. On the right side, toward the south, is the palace which they say that Solomon built. Within it are stables, so huge that they can hold more than two thousand horses or 1,500 camels, and near this palace the Templar knights have many great houses and there are also the foundations of a great new church which is not yet finished. This order has enormous property and endless revenues in this region and in other places. This allows them to give alms to the poor, though not as a tithe, as the Hospitallers do. The order also has many knights for the defense of the land of the Christians.

Benefits of Membership

Player characters who join the Knights Templar receive a few bonus abilities. The Templar Knights were fanatic in their quest to destroy the Saracens. Consequently, all characters who are members of this order receive a +2 Attack Bonus against Muslims.

The knights were also the earliest bankers in Western culture. While individual knights take a vow of chastity, the organization is very well funded. ***Thus, a member of the Knights Templar may make a Charisma check at a base DC of 15 to have the order purchase him a piece of equipment. For every 50 gold over 100 that the item costs, the DC increases by 1.*** In essence, the knight simply has to convince his superior that he needs the equipment. If he can pull it off, the order will get it for him.

Chapter 3: Knights of St. John of the Hospital

The Knights of St. John the Hospitaller were among the most important of all knightly orders during the Middle Ages. This was due to the extent of the order's area of control and because of its duration and strength. The power of the organization extended both spiritually and physically throughout the Holy Land. To that end, the Hospitallers could deny or grant access to the Middle East, declaring it "too dangerous" for some. Additionally, they were very closely tied to the pope and in his favor. With this sort of influence they were able to manipulate the countries of Europe to their ends.

The Knights of St. John, also called the Hospitaller Knights, were an order that loosely existed before the Crusades and found their home when Jerusalem was captured by the Christian armies. The Hospitaller Knights have been known by several different names throughout their history: the Hospitallers of Jerusalem until 1309; the members were called Knights of Rhodes from 1309 until 1522; and the Knights of Malta (technically a splinter group, covered in detail in another section of this book) after 1530.

The origins of the order is difficult to determine and is obfuscated by many different tales and legends. It is known for certain that the Hospitallers' founder was a man named Gerald or Gerard, whose birthplace and family name is completely undocumentable. One of the few papers that legitimizes his title as founder of the Hospitaller Knights is a far more modern piece than the history of the order would suggest: a papal Bull dated 1113, addressed to Geraudo institutori ac praeposito Hirosolimitani Xenodochii.

Even before the Crusades, hostelries and hospitals were used to shelter pilgrims who flocked to the Holy Places, and the Knights who guarded and worked in such places were seen as holy men. The peasants considered such individuals to be touched by God; their generosity and knowledge of medicine saved lives, and their prayers were unceasing, even for the most deeply wounded or sick.

The order of the Hospitallers of St. John originated in Jerusalem at the end of the 11th Century. The knights who attended the hospices there dedicated their lives to keeping the peace and tending the sick, giving up all material possessions and taking vows of chastity and fidelity to their brother knights.

The first Hospitaller monastery began as a hospice, and the knights dedicated their lives to the care of sick and weary pilgrims visiting the Holy Land.

Although historians do not know the precise date of the hospice's founding, it is certain that the monastery was independently running by the time the first Crusaders arrived in Jerusalem in 1099. It cared for the sick and wounded knights, and made many inroads to stability by caring for wealthy and noble men, who subsequently became patrons to their order.

The Hospitallers were not constrained to the Holy Land but spread their mercy and their medicinal knowledge throughout Europe where it was needed. A Frankish hospice is written of in the time of Charlemagne, and several prominent Frankish nobles owed their lives to the Hospitallers. Another well-known Hospitaller location was within Hungary, where the knights had a large stone building for their purposes. There, the Knights Hospitaller had the ear of the Hungarian King, Stephen, who supported their activities and considered them to be the most blessed of knightly orders.

Mottoes and Words of Honor

In many of the texts which remain, there is mention of the Hospitallers tending not only the sick or the wounded but also spending their time among the poor. They also used their resources to offer hospitality and safe haven to travelers and strangers. According to these manuscripts, Gerard believed very much in caring for the soul of the individual as well as the body, and his epitaph defines his work: "Pauperibus servus, pius hospitibus . . . . Undique collegit pasceret unde sous." – Poor slave, devout stranger; from all sides he has gathered them together to a place where they might be nourished.

In Italy, another famous Hospitaller location, controlled by the merchants of Amalfi, served the public. The knights of Italy were far more merchant-oriented and possessed a significant amount of money despite their vows of poverty. The Italian hospice was dedicated to St. John of Alexandria, and their patron was St. Augustine (rather than St. Benedict), further separating them from their brothers in the main body of the Knights Hospitaller. The hospice of Amalfi wasn't a stand-alone sanctuary. It relied far more on the money that came in from the merchant class. Rather than seeking out the sick and injured, they accepted those that were sent by their merchant sponsors.

The monastery run by Gerard in the Holy Land profited from the presence of the crusaders. Crusades were good for business, bringing many nobles to pray at the altar of the Hospitallers, and creating a great deal of sick and wounded men that needed the tender care of the Hospitallers. Since they accepted "donations" for their services, war was a profitable business. The Knights of Gerard lived on the gratitude of their subjects, using their battlefield prowess only when necessary to rescue an injured individual (usually someone of great importance) from the field. These revenues were used to acquire territory for new monasteries and hospices not only in the new Kingdom of Jerusalem, but in Europe.

History

After Gerard founded the Knights Hospitaller, his successor, Raymond of Provence (1120-60), caused the erection of more spacious buildings near the Church of the Holy Sepulchre. These larger hospices could hold more than three times the number of individuals as the earlier buildings, showing not only the Hospitallers' new prosperity, but also the great need for their services within the Holy Land. The hospices needed individuals to tend them, and, thus, the Knights Hospitaller began to openly recruit young and intelligent men into their order.

The Sword of Holy Peace

The Sword of Holy Peace is a +2 Holy longsword and conforms to the following stats:

Damage: 1d8 (Subdual Damage only) (plus Holy Damage of 1d6, also Subdual)

Crit: None

Range: —

Weight: 3 lb

Type: Slashing

The Sword of Holy Peace is not a fighter's weapon, nor was it ever intended to be used in war. It is a slender blade on a pale silver hilt, apparently too fragile to truly cause harm. The sword is a holy relic and bestows one Negative Level on any Evil creature that attempts to wield it. The Negative Level remains as long as the creature holds the weapon and disappears when the weapon is cast away.

All damage dealt by the Sword of Holy Peace is delivered instead to the wielder. The sword is a weapon of peace and will not retain an edge to its blade. If the sword is placed upon someone's shoulder, the wielder will suffer hits per round of concentration as though attacked by the sword, and the penitent will receive double that amount of hit points of healing. The hits suffered by the wielder take the form of stigmata, not open wounds, and the wielder will possess a holy glow throughout his or her body while performing this healing.

They taught skills with the blade and also with medicine and finances, helping these young monk-knights learn how to care for their patients as well as defend the monasteries that sheltered them.

The Hospitallers of Jerusalem were the first group of Knights Hospitaller, and from their origins came all other such groups. Their primary oaths were those of fidelity, chastity, and fraternity, but, as the group grew larger and their holdings increased, they created a new law to help govern their increasing number. This law was called the Rule of Provence, and it dealt with the conduct of monks of the Hospitallers as religious doctors and caregivers and did not in any way mention them as knights or soldiers. The Rule attempts to leave behind the more violent aspects of the knightly order, replacing it entirely with their positions as servitors within the hospitals and hospices. The Rule is very clear, and well defined, stating that each hospital maintained by the Hospitallers of St. John shall permanently maintain no less than five physicians and three surgeons – all paid for by donations and alms gathered in the hospice or through begging on the street for the common good.

The brothers of the knighthood – now demoted to mere monks – were ordered by the Rule of Provence to dedicate their lives to healing others. This rule was taken very seriously by several of the monastery hospices, whose members laid down their swords and ceased teaching new initiates how to fight or defend themselves. The writings of an educated pilgrim to the Holy Land in 1150 records one such hospital, and mentions that more than 2000 sick individuals were cared for in the hospice at one time – an obviously exaggerated number since so many people ill in one place would have certainly been the result of a plague or other such devastation and not simply from the day-to-day industry of even a city as large as Jerusalem.

Those members of the Knights Hospitaller who did not choose to lay down their swords were given other duties that took them far from the monasteries. These knights were tasked to raise funds for the hospices so that they could buy needed equipment and supplies to continue the "good work." They served as escorts and safeguards in the Holy Land, guiding travelers and pilgrims through dangerous and difficult areas in order to keep them safe. These knights accompanied and defended pilgrims, taking any injured or sick to the hospices so that the medicinal practitioners of the monasteries could tend to their needs. These knight-escorts quickly became an integral part of society in the Holy Land, and wealthy merchants or nobles did not often travel without them. This led to a vast increase in funds for the Knights Hospitallers, and they quickly raised their membership. Soon, the Knights Hospitallers were affluent, their forces reaching the size of a small army and their hospitals expanding to three times their original size. And still their coffers swelled.

Battle

Although the Knights Hospitaller were not a purely militant group, they were often seen on the field of battle, rescuing the wounded and helping the badly injured die in peace and with God's forgiveness. The Knights Hospitaller recruited from natives of the area, asking peasants and other locals to help them find the sick and injured so that they could be treated; in so doing, they expanded their knowledge of both war craft and medicinal healing with local flavor.

Most of the Knights Hospitaller units served as light cavalry, armed in the Turkish fashion with little armor and swift steeds. They used cavalry sabers rather than broadswords, and their goal on the battlefield was best served with quick strikes rather than long-term engagements. Their primary battle-commander was the Knight Marshal, whose duties included complete command of the militant Knight Hospitallers, as well as fighting on the battlefield himself. No member of the Knights Hospitaller commanded from the side of the field; the entire order fought side by side, giving their lives in the defense of one another. This made them very different than ordinary secular knights, who rarely risked their lives if they did not see direct personal gain.

Many of the Grand Masters of the Knights Hospitaller were also Knight Marshals, and the records of the Knights Hospitaller are filled with Grand Masters who perished on the battlefields of Jerusalem. A marked distinction is made between secular knights, who served in battle only for a short time, and the Knights Hospitaller, who remained on the battlefield until the last wounded man was retrieved.

While the Hospitallers enjoyed the height of their prosperity and glory, they controlled vast tracts of land in both the Holy Land and in Europe. Hospitallers possessed no fewer than seven strongholds, including keeps in the cities of Margat, Krals, and Tripoli. They enjoyed the revenues of more than 140 estates as well as the constant influx of money gathered by escorting pilgrims on their journey to and from the holy city of Jerusalem. In Europe, they controlled more than twenty separate estates, some of which were used as hospices while others were

The Sword of Holy Peace (cont'd)

Targets affected by the Sword of Holy Peace feel an overwhelming compulsion to aid and serve the Church and the Order of the Knights Hospitaller for a number of days equal to 1/4 the number of wounds healed by the Sword of Holy Peace. Beneficiaries are not mindless automatons of the Church but instead are loyal subjects and earnestly offer aid to God's servants. This does not mean they will risk their lives for no cause, but it does make them loyal to a fault while under the continuing effects of the sword.

The Sword of Holy Peace can never be used on Chaotic Evil creatures. In these instances, the sword simply does not heal the recipient.

Rivalry

While the Order of St. John was a mixed order of militant knights and medicinal monks, the Knights Templar began and continued to be a purely military order from their founding. The two groups were politically opposed (even though their professed loyalties were to the same cause) from the beginning. The Templars followed a different monastic rule and wore a different robe – a white habit with a red cross, while the Hospitallers wore a black mantle with a white cross. The two orders were clearly distinguished both on the field and within the city of Jerusalem, and many historians believe there was open division – if not occasional hidden warfare – between the two groups. They soon became open rivals, and this rivalry increased the sharp decline and instability of the Kingdom of Jerusalem.

The two orders independently influenced the decisions of both Church and State heads. They were recognized as regular orders and were endowed by the papacy with extensive privileges, absolute independence from all spiritual and temporal authority save that of Rome, exemptions from tithes, and had the right to have their own chapels, clergy, and cemeteries. Because of their oaths, both groups were charged with the military defense of the Holy Land by papal decree, and neither one could override the other's authority. This led to a vicious rivalry between them, a division which split the Holy Land in half and allowed a breach in the defense of Jerusalem that eventually led to its fall.

for unification and record-keeping (actually controlled by less militant members of the order whose responsibility it was to maintain its prestigious position among the courts of Europe).

The Knights Hospitaller soon became so wealthy that they organized a financial plan to maintain and collect the revenues of their widely scattered possessions. Although the Knights Hospitaller (and their monastic branches) were bound to poverty, their adherence to this oath slipped and was easily corrupted by the wealth and prosperity of their lands.

By 1120, the Order of the Knights Hospitaller began to take on a more military role within the Holy Land. They believed that to defend the pilgrims (as they had been charged by the Rule of Provence), they must safeguard the roads upon which they traveled. Therefore, they began a small crusade of their own – seizing and acquiring many castles along the roadways to Jerusalem from Europe. These fortresses were primarily taken from Muslim "infidels" and then retooled to Christian concepts and made to serve the needs of the order.

From these keeps, the Knights Hospitaller defended the territory captured by the Crusaders from Muslim attackers, maintained the roads to Europe, and kept the pilgrims safe from Muslim attack. At first, mercenary soldiers were employed to fight for them, but as their order grew more and more prosperous, the army of the Knights Hospitaller grew and the order assumed complete control of all military activity. By the 13th Century, the Rule of Provence was all but forgotten, and the Hospitallers abandoned many of their hospices and hospitals for keeps and military movements. Although they maintained small hospices within their military garrisons, the order turned its back on much of the activity that it was founded to achieve.

The fall of the Holy Land affected the Knights Hospitaller dramatically. Without their power base in Jerusalem, they lost much of their political standing and many of their financial vaults. After the fall of Acre (the last of the Crusader states) in 1291, the Knights were forced to leave the Holy Land. Their major keeps along the road to Jerusalem were besieged and mostly destroyed, and the Knights Hospitaller Order lost more than one-half its total membership. Those remaining Knights seized as much of their gathered wealth as possible, and relocated to the island of Cyprus. In 1312, the Templars were dissolved and the Hospitallers, the sole remaining military order in the East, felt the need for a more stable base from which to carry out military and naval activities in the Eastern Mediterranean. Jerusalem was in Saracen hands, who remembered the activities of the Knights Hospitaller and their attack and seizure of Muslim keeps along the roadways into the Holy Lands. The Knights Hospitaller were one of the most hated groups in the Middle East, and most of the fanatic Muslim groups targeted them for destruction. The Holy Land was no longer safe for their order.

Using their massive political and financial resources in Europe, the order was able to survive the fall of the Kingdom of Jerusalem. They retained only their possessions in Tripoli and a few other captured Muslim strongholds, but even these were lost to them when Acre fell. Only by fleeing the Holy Land could the order survive, and in the Kingdom of Cyprus they found a safe haven. However, moving to an island nation required the order to alter its military and political strategy, and many of it members learned seagoing warfare, using their newly created navy as protection. They equipped fleets to fight the Muslims on the sea and to protect those pilgrims who still sought to visit Jerusalem and. other holy sites on the mainland. But it was chiefly the conquest of the Island of Rhodes, under the Grand Master Foulques de Villaret, that brought about a complete transformation of the order.

Armor of the Knights of St. John of the Hospital

Type: Full Plate Armor

AC Bonus: +9 (+8 base, +1 enchantment)

Max Dex Bonus: +3

Armor Check Penalty: -3

Arcane Spell Failure: 25%

Speed: 40 feet

Weight: 30 lb

This magical suit of armor was purportedly given to the first chaplain of the Order of St. John by a vision of the Virgin Mary. It has since been worn by the Grand Master of the order or, on rare occasion, by a Champion or other prestigious member, in particular during the period of time when the order served in Northern Europe and the Holy Land was no longer under Christian control. Although the armor seems light and somewhat frail, it is tougher than steel and can absorb even the harshest blow. The armor is considered one of the most sacred relics of the Hospitaller order and is protected and cared for with almost religious respect. It is never worn except in formal court or on the battlefield.

The Knights of Rhodes (1309-1522)

The Knights of Rhodes, successors of the Hospitallers of St. John, may have seemed like a branch of the original knightly order, but in fact they were vastly different both in organization and in their goals. They controlled the Island of Rhodes completely, using their power and wealth to purchase it outright from the Kingdom of Cyprus. In this manner, the leader of the order was also the King of Rhodes, and granted the secular rights of a king in all ways. The fact that he was also a monk and a knight of their order was inconsequential to the Knights of Rhodes, who saw this as a necessary political diversion in order

Armor of the Knights of St. John of the Hospital (cont'd)

The armor is a dark grey in color, forged from the finest steel and inlaid with pale silver and white tracings across the shoulders and breastplate. The front plate of the armor is emblazoned with the white cross of the Knights Hospitaller.

The armor is exceptionally forged of very light plates and weighs much less than ordinary plate mail. Further, it is enchanted to allow speedy recovery of the injured; the armor will not slow down the movement of the one wearing it but may actually increase his movement rate.

to give their order the stability it desperately needed to survive.

The most important step taken on this new road was their merger with another order: their old rivals, the Knights Templar. The two orders each lost a significant amount of power and wealth from the fall of Jerusalem and the wars in the Holy Lands, and, in order to survive as a military organization, they worked together to stabilize their position. In 1312, the Knights Templar and the Knights Hospitaller no longer existed; only the new Order of the Knights of Rhodes fought to preserve the Holy Land.

After their military rout from the Holy Land, the Knights of Rhodes turned completely away from their order's original mission to help the sick and injured. Although they built a new infirmary next to their military keep on the island, they were not utterly devoted to the care of the sick or of pilgrims. Such things took a distinctly secondary place as the members of the order were too busy re-forging their nature and stabilizing their holdings in Europe and in the Holy Land. The "Hospitaller" name was dropped altogether, and a new sovereignty took precedence over old goals.

To recognize the new order of knights and to help their financial situation, the pope assigned the Knights of Rhodes significant property in every country except Aragon and Portugal. At this time the organization took its definitive form, the whole body being divided into tongues, priories, and commanderies. Each nation (of the eight) possessed its own ruling government headed by a bailiff whose title was independent of the order, and who was assigned by the Knighthood within that nation.

The Knights of Rhodes took their new duties very seriously and soon became one of the most feared pirate groups in the Middle East. They pillaged and plundered Muslim ports, including Constantinople and many of the wealthiest coastal cities in the Orient. They were known as "corsairs," knights of the sea, and they practiced a constant scourge against the Muslim wealth that flowed through the silk and spice trade of the Middle East. To their benefit, they also defended Christian holdings and ships, escorting them as faithfully as their predecessors escorted pilgrims through the Holy Land.

But the revenge of the Knights of Rhodes against the Muslims of the Holy Land was not destined to last very long. A new power in the Muslim lands rose, giving impressive support to their shipping lines and authorizing newer and faster fleets of ships in order to destroy these Christian pirates. The Ottoman Turks turned their eyes toward more than simply destroying the Knights of Rhodes one ship at a time; they planned an outright assault against Rhodes itself, blockading the island and burning the ported ships in order to seal in the knights and force their eventual surrender. In 1522, Solyman II of the Ottomans launched a massive fleet against Rhodes. He came with more than 400 ships and an army of 140,000 men committed to battling or starving the Knights of Rhodes into submission. The island sustained this great onslaught for a period of six months and capitulated only when their supplies were completely exhausted.

Owing to their great bravery and due to the clever negotiation of their surrender, Solyman spared the lives of the knights on the island. They were permitted to withdraw, and Solyman even lent them his ships to return to Europe – homage to their bravery and the fact that the Knights of Rhodes were worthy foes. Afterwards, the last of the knights dispersed to the other nations of Europe, broken and defeated. Their livelihoods were destroyed, their power and prestige seriously injured by this great loss.

The Knights of Malta (1530-1798)

After their demoralizing defeat at the hands of the Turks, the Knights of Rhodes were grudgingly granted a keep on the island of Malta. It was not an independent nation like Rhodes was but instead owed allegiance and fealty to the King of Spain and his feudal state of Sicily. Still, the knights used this minor victory to bolster their courage, and they renamed their order accordingly – the Knights of Malta were born.

The Knights of Malta at once resumed the manner of life they had already practiced for two centuries at Rhodes. With a fleet which did not number more than seven galleys they resisted the Barbary pirates who infested the western basin of the Mediterranean. The Knights of Malta were also permitted to equip galleys at their own expense to give chase to the Turks. These enterprises did not fail to draw upon them fresh attacks from the Ottomans. Solyman II, regretting his generosity, gathered for a second time all the forces of his empire to dislodge the Christian corsairs from their retreat. The siege of Malta, quite as famous as that of Rhodes, lasted for four months in 1565. The Turks had already taken possession of a part of the island, destroying nearly the whole of the old city and slaying half the knights and almost 8000 soldiers, when Malta was delivered by an army of relief from Spain. In retreating the Turks are said to have left 30,000 dead. A new city had to be built: the present city of Valette, so named in memory of its valiant grand master who had sustained this siege. Malta, however, was not rid of its most dangerous adversary until the battle of Lepanto (1571) which dealt the Ottoman fleet a fatal and final blow.

Organization

The organization of the Knights Hospitaller changed dramatically throughout the order's long history. During their period within the Holy Land, the order progressed from a military order to a balanced divide between a dual-faction order of monks and knights-at-arms, and then, when the order reached Rhodes, it altered again and became solely militant. These changes affected the organization, finances, and leadership of the group. In many ways, the Knights Hospitaller are not at all the same knights throughout history, and their structure clearly reflects these violent and drastic changes in their philosophy.

Initially, members of the Order of the Knights Hospitaller joined the group as martial reserves. Because they were taught full discipline as military men as well as the modesty and

Shield of the Knights Hospitaller

Type: Large Metal Shield

AC Bonus: +3 (+2 base, +1 enchantment)

Armor Check Penalty: 0

Arcane Spell Failure: 5%

Weight: 5 lb

This shield is painted with the formal badge of the Knights Hospitaller. The shield offers its cover bonus to anyone within a 10-foot radius who is either a member of the Knights Hospitaller or is being actively protected or treated by a member of the order.

worship of the monks, they were divided into various structured units, which fought, ate, exercised, and prayed together.

Later, the brothers of the knightly order began to separate according to the lines of their interests and abilities – the Hospitallers, medicinal units, and doctors became their own unit, as did the more militant soldiers. The other factions also segregated, until the order was completely broken down into feudal-like hierarchy. The first class is comprised of the professed religious men, those completely dedicated to serving God and little else. These were few and far between, and this classification rapidly died out as the others grew. The vast majority of the members of the early Hospitallers were relegated to the second and third classes – the mediciners and the soldiers.

There were six ranks within the order. These were:

Bailiff Grand Cross

Knight of Justice, Knight of Grace, Sub-Prelate, Chaplain

Commander Brother

Officer Brother, Sub-Chaplain

Serving Brother

Esquire, Donat

Bailiffs and Knights of Justice and Grace are the superior officers within a monastery or keep. Typically, a Bailiff controls the knights of an entire nation, where a Knight of Justice controls a single keep or land area. A Knight of Justice may be in charge of more than one keep or area, if the Bailiff of the nation feels that the Knight of Justice is adequate and capable to handle more than one such large estate.

A Knight of Grace is essentially the same rank as a Knight of Justice, but the two posts differ in nobility and external prestige. In order to qualify for the title of Knight of Justice, the individual must posses either paternal nobility or the right to bear a properly recorded coat-of-arms. The only practical difference between the two ranks is that a Knight of Justice is allowed two personal squires whereas the Knights of Grace may only have one.

Alternate Titles

Each nation (of the eight that housed the Knights Hospitallers) possessed its own ruling government headed by a bailiff whose title was independent of the order and assigned by the Knighthood within that nation. In Provence, the national leader of the Knights of Rhodes was the Grand Commander; in Auvergne, he was the Marshal; in France, he was known as the Grand Hospitaller; in Italy, Admiral; in Aragon, the leader was the Standard-Bearer; to Castile, the Grand Chancellor; in Germany, Grand Bailiff; to England, where the national leader of the Knights of Rhodes was the Turcoplier. The grand master, complete overlord of the entire knightly order, might be elected from any of the various nations.

The Three Orders

Within the later versions of the Knights Hospitaller order, there were three distinct classes of members. Of these, the military brothers and the brothers infirmarian were the two most important. The brothers chaplain, to whom was entrusted the divine service, formed a third class, but they were not segregated as the others were. While a military knight lived apart from the true hospitaller arm of the order, the chaplains were allowed to live with and operate in either of the others' territory, changing their locations as they saw fit in the service of God and by the leave of their commander.

Promotions within the three orders were made primarily on the basis of service. If a member distinguishes himself or herself towards the order, promotion to the rank of officer brother or sister may follow after one year, although in most cases it takes four to 10 years. Promotion to the rank of commander may follow for an average of one third of the officers and also takes from four to 10 years. Particularly distinguished and prominent members and those who have served the order outstandingly for many years, may be promoted to Knight of Justice or Knight of Grace; however, only a small percentage of the membership ever made it to these lofty posts.

A Knight of the Order

The standard Knight Hospitaller was a noble descended as the third or later son of his family and destined to be an absent member of his family line. In order to keep the lines of succession free of argument, most noble families kept their eldest son close, made their second son a priest, and then sent any other male offspring to war.

Most Knights Hospitaller wear their robes or habits at all times, but some prefer to wear the robes of a doctor or the chain mail of a soldier, particularly as the order fragmented into these two separate groups. The Knights Hospitaller had finer garb than most other orders because their clothing was more frequently replaced (bloodstains and rips occurred so frequently in the medicinal faction that an entire group of seamstresses were kept on staff to do nothing but repair the doctor's garb).

Arms of St. John the Hospitaller

Traditionally, the Knights Hospitaller wore a black surcoat emblazoned with a white cross; the style of this cross became known as "maltese" in the later days of their order. All members of the order may wear this blazon on their robes, cloaks, or painted upon their shields. A more elaborate version of the icon was known as the badge. Bailiffs, Knights, Dames and Chaplains, displayed on their shields the full badge of the Order, so that they could be distinguished from a mere soldier-at-arms. The cross of the order is a very distinctive figure, shaped like a white star of eight points. As a badge, the cross is embellished at each of the four angles with the alternating figures of a *lion passant guardant* and a *unicorn passant.*

The Knights chose the shape of the cross to represent the spiritual qualities blessed by Christ in the Sermon on the Mount. The four arms of the cross represent the four virtues of Christ: Prudence, Justice, Temperance, and Fortitude. The eight points within those cross-arms represent the eight Beatitudes, and it is white in order to represent the purity of the soul.

How Do I Join?

The conditions for admission to the Knights Hospitaller order include that the petitioner must be of at least one-sixteenth noble birth, must practice the Catholic Faith, and be of full legal age. Once a candidate has proven these facts to be true, he is tested by the Knights in order to prove his integrity of character and strength of will and conviction.

Final admission to the order is subject to numerous small conditions, a willingness to swear the oath of the order, and a paid entrance fee of 900 marks. During the first four years as an acolyte (or squire), the brother is considered to be on probation. After this tenure is complete, he will be allowed to swear the oaths of knighthood and formally join the Knights Hospitaller.

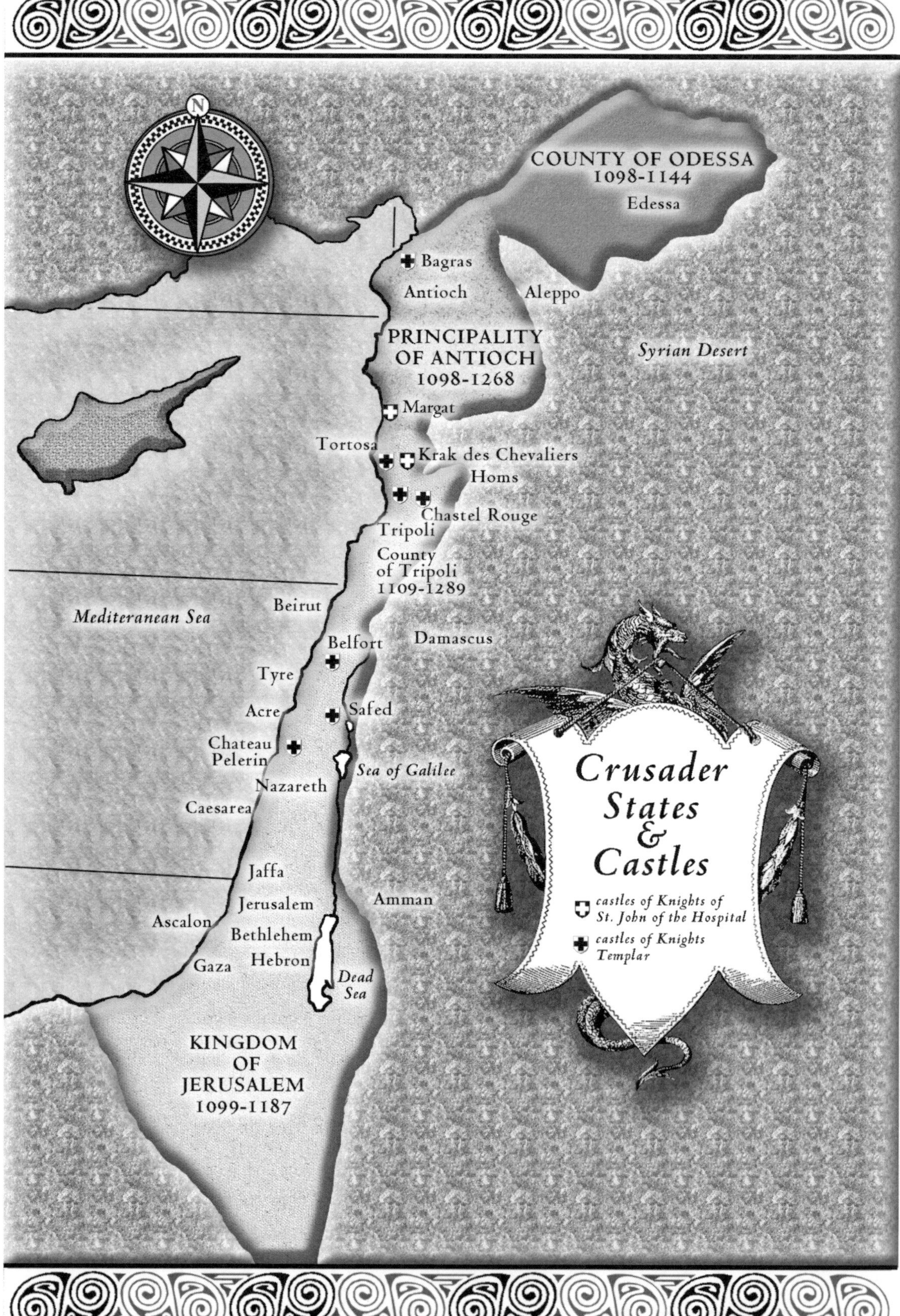

N
COUNTY OF ODESSA
1098-1144
Edessa
Bagras
Antioch
Aleppo
PRINCIPALITY
OF ANTIOCH
1098-1268
Syrian Desert
Margat
Tortosa
Krak des Chevaliers
Homs
Chastel Rouge
Tripoli
County
of Tripoli
1109-1289
Mediteranean Sea
Beirut
Belfort
Damascus
Tyre
Acre
Safed
Chateau
Pelerin
Sea of Galilee
Nazareth
Caesarea
Jaffa
Jerusalem
Amman
Ascalon
Bethlehem
Gaza
Hebron
Dead
Sea
KINGDOM
OF
JERUSALEM
1099-1187
Crusader
States
&
Castles
castles of Knights of
St. John of the Hospital
castles of Knights
Templar

Benefits of Membership

Members of the Order of St. John gain a +4 Class Bonus to all Heal checks. Knights of the order also gain a +2 Class Bonus to all Will Saves.

Chapter 4: The Knights of Santiago

Many knights in the Middle Ages were kept from maintaining normal lives outside their orders, but it was not so with the Spanish Knights of Santiago. These knights were encouraged to maintain families, political ties, and other obligations outside the order while still remaining faithful to the tenets and the brotherhood of their code.

Initially, the Order of Santiago was created by 12 knights who referred to themselves as *los caballeros de Cáceres.* They were simply noblemen who swore an oath against all banditry and felonies and who used their strength and their swords to defend the pilgrims that traveled to the holy site of Santiago de Compostela. In 1161, the King of León, Fernando II called them to his court, offering them numerous accolades if they would join his personal guard. The knights refused, politely saying that they best served the king by serving his people. Pleased with their loyalty and their stalwart sense of duty, King Fernando knighted them formally and created them as a knightly order, instituting upon them the formal title of the Order of Santiago.

In 1174, the order was unified within the city of Uclés, and the Knights of Santiago at last had a capital. They were sponsored by numerous Castilian kings, and kept close ties with the Spanish government and nobility. The order took part in the Castilian Civil Wars, and finally, unified with the noblemen who had initially sponsored them, the King of Castile was named the master of the Order of Santiago.

For the next few centuries, the Knights of Santiago was the most distinguished of all Spanish knighthood orders, equivalent to the Musketeers in France or the Knights of the Garter in England. Indeed, the Knights of Santiago became one of the largest orders of knights in Spain, numbering over 700,000 members in good standing. The Knight of Santiago made several oaths upon becoming a full member of the order and was expected to live up to the highest standards. However, one vow was distinctly different than those taken by other orders. Instead of swearing to poverty, fidelity, and chastity, the Knights of Santiago swore only to keep "marital chastity," therefore, to keep themselves with only one woman within the bonds of marriage rather than refusing all sex outright. The Knights of Santiago primarily cared for the well-being of the poor and peasant citizens of Spain, but they also provided hospital services as much as was possible. Like the Teutonic Knights, the order also is commanded to undertake the evangelization of all those who do not yet know God.

History

The Order of Santiago (to the English, "Saint Iago" or Saint James), is more properly titled the "Military Order of Saint James of the Sword" as they were initially christened by the King of Castile. Their initial purpose was to provide protection for the pilgrims traveling to and from the tomb of Saint James at Compostella, the most important pilgrimage center in Western Europe. Sadly, this tomb is located very near the border with the Muslim

The Sword of Martyrdom

The Sword of Martyrdom is a +2 Holy longsword, and conforms to the following stats:

Damage: 1d8 (plus Holy Damage of 2d6)

Crit: 19-20 x2

Range: —

Weight: 3 lbs

Type: Slashing

The Sword of Martyrdom bestows one Negative Level on any Evil creature that attempts to wield it. The Negative Level remains as long as the creature holds the weapon and disappears when the weapon is no longer wielded.

The Sword of Martyrdom is a powerful weapon in the hands of a defender and is designed to allow for a "final stand" against an overwhelming enemy. When wielded by a Paladin, the Sword of Martyrdom gains an additional +1 to attack rolls and +2 to damage for each enemy directly facing him or her. Up to 10 total assailants may be faced at any one time. If the character is defending a holy site against intrusion, he or she gains an additional 25 Hit Points and a +4 Circumstance Bonus to AC while wielding the sword.

The Sword of Martyrdom can never be used against ordained and sanctified priests of the Catholic Church, nor will it harm innocents unless they are attacking the wielder. It will also not harm members of the Order of Santiago, and the master of that Order may call the blade into his hand from any point in the world so long as the sword is not broken or sheathed in iron.

lands of southern Spain, and those who dared the long and treacherous journey were frequently harassed and attacked, even killed, by Moorish bandits. Between 1164 and 1170, the 12 founding knights of the order attached themselves to the many churches and monasteries surrounding the tomb so that they could make the roads safe for travelers and pilgrims.

The knights were taken in by the priests and monks residing in those monasteries, trading the promise of military protection for the comfort and solitude of the monastic life. These new knights also adopted the monastic rule of Saint Augustine – to live a pious and faithful life and dedicate their swords and service to God. The knights brought a considerable endowment, being noble by birth (and many of them wealthy), and also unified their blades to fight against the more serious and dangerous threats on the roads of Spain. Within a few years, the monks no longer looked upon them as intruders into their quiet havens but instead shared their common revenues and agreed to provide hospital services to the knights, their serving brothers, and sick pilgrims.

The fledgling order immediately attempted to obtain the support of King Ferdinand of Aragon, and his response was very favorable. In 1171, Ferdinand granted the knights title to their original headquarters in the town of Caceres. Over the next two years, the knights swelled rapidly, destroying countless Muslim invaders and bandits, and seizing the towns of Badajoz, Mora (near Toledo), and Fuentiduena (near Aranjuez). In 1174, they were granted the castle of Uclés by King Alfonso IX of Castile, where they established their principal seat and the capital of their order.

Over the next ten years, the order grew even more rapidly than before. They founded hospitals at Toledo, Avíla and Talavera, and opened a leper hospital at Villa San Martín, near Carion. A grateful King of Castile (and now Portugal) granted the order several extensive properties in Portugal and later acquired properties in France, Italy, Palestine, Carinthia, Hungary, and England (given them by grateful pilgrims).

War

Unfortunately, the Christian Kingdoms of Spain were often unstable, and political factions tore at the throne of Castile and Aragon almost to the point of overthrowing the entire kingdom. Knights and their orders found themselves frequently placed between two feuding rulers, being used as pawns in a larger power struggle. Their loyalty was often questioned by the constantly shifting tides of politics, and more than one honorable knight was put to death simply for following the wrong leader at the wrong time.

These constantly shifting loyalties further weakened the Christian cause, delaying their ultimate victory over the Moors and ruining several of the advances made by the Knights of Santiago on their own. Making the best of the situation, the order rapidly assumed extensive feudal powers that were dropped during the power struggles of feuding nobles. They collected taxes, kept the peace and upheld the laws wherever possible, and, in doing so, the Knights of Santiago collected several new estates and filled their own coffers to a great extent. Their widespread power became more evident, and they were hailed in many provinces as the heroes of the people of Spain.

Yet being a hero was dangerous in the political tides of such an unstable kingdom. When the Knights of Santiago acquired new estates or established a political hold over some part of a province, their first action was always made with an eye to the defense of such holdings. The knights built walls, created moats and other protections, and in larger towns, built substantial fortresses to help protect the common person from the relentless invasions of petty, power-hungry minor nobles. Each of the principal castles would necessarily have their own administrative systems, subordinate to the local Commander, with groups of knights, sergeants, and foot soldiers.

Because (in general) the Knights of Santiago were allied closely with the King of Castile, they received several gifts from the throne. These monetary stipends helped cover the costs of their knightly territories and assisted them in more closely protecting the king. Their armor was always of the best quality, and their scattered territories regularly paid taxes to the throne – taxes used to stabilize the King of Castile within the constantly changing political scheme.

Unfortunately, the distance from the central leadership contributed to divisions within the order because some areas were peaceful and others constantly under political or actual siege from enemies within the kingdom. This led to a great amount of division in the order, and each keep or estate was forced to take a very individualistic, independent view of their order's purposes and goals. A further aspect of the organization's responsibilities – and one which was likewise consigned to Calatrava and Alcántara – was assisting in resettling land captured from the Moors with Christian populations from the north – something that few of the compounds of knights were able to accomplish as the strife in Castile grew ever greater.

In 1195, the knights suffered a bitter defeat at Alarcos; their Grand Master was fatally wounded and many of their number killed. This was a cruel blow to the proud Knights of Santiago, for their ultimate goal – to restore Christian order to the Muslim lands – seemed a failure. Internal war broke out soon after, and the knights separated into two independent groups, both claiming to be the "true" Order of Santiago. The knights elected two Masters, and went to war over which one would reclaim the other's holdings and loyal servitors. This internal faction war within the Knights of Santiago devastated their prestige, their holdings, and their honor within the courts of Castile. It ended in the death of one of the Grand Masters and the submission of all the Knights of Santiago to a man named Gonzálo Ordóñez in 1203.

Over the course of the next century, the knights were engaged in war with both Moors and fellow Christians, generally supporting the kings of Castile. They redeemed their original purpose – to fight back the Moors and Muslims from Spanish borders and add to the territories of the King of Castile. They were

Armor of the Knights of Santiago

Type: Full Plate Armor

AC Bonus: +10 (+8 base, +2 enchantment)

Max Dex Bonus: +3

Armor Check Penalty: -3

Arcane Spell Failure: 25%

Speed: 20 ft

Weight: 30 lb

This magical suit of armor was created for the Knights of Santiago by the King of Spain's finest smiths. Unlike many orders, the Knights of Santiago rarely bring out this treasure from their armory; it is considered to be a great prize, and its power is not often called upon. Three members of the order are given the responsibility to protect, clean, and guard it, and only those members can wear it if there is true need.

The armor is dark gold in color, forged from strange materials that reflect the golden light of the sun. Over this base, it is inlaid with black and red tracings across the shoulders and breastplate and the symbols of flowers across both wrists. The front plate of the armor is emblazoned with the red cross of the Knights of Santiago, and this emblem seems to be created of blood, spilled on the front of the armor as if spun from Christ's own wounds. When the knight within the armor is wounded, the cross grows brighter, absorbing the wearer's injuries. The knight gains an additional +1 Circumstance Bonus to his Strength Modifier for each 15 Hit Points lost while wearing the armor. If the knight is healed, this bonus vanishes proportionately.

highly successful, possibly because the knights who argued with the new Grand Master's plan for the war found themselves quickly placed on the front lines. As the Moors were steadily driven southwards, the Knights of Santiago acquired more extensive territories and increased their numbers despite the ever increasing rumbles and quarrels between the militant knights and the religious brothers and sisters of their order.

In 1312, the knights built a convent in Seville, designed to become the new center of command for their unruly order. They signed a formal alliance with the King of Castile once more in order to receive the territory for their new keep, but the Crown was increasingly anxious to strengthen its control over this powerful, and potentially disloyal, military organization. The Knights of Santiago were unpredictable, their politics as violent and ever-changing as the nobles against whom they fought only a few decades before.

When the Grand Master of the order died with no clear successor, King Alfonso XI persuaded the knights to elect one of his natural (that is, bastard) sons, the 10-year-old Don Fernándo, as Grand Master. This edict required Papal dispensation, but the knights received the pope's blessing (primarily due to the myriad and expensive gifts the King's envoys brought on their visit to him). However, on the death of the king soon thereafter, relations between the knights and the Crown deteriorated again. The new king's first act was to command the execution of Alfonso XI's mistress, the mother of the Grand Master of the Knights of Santiago. The new king further commanded the deposition of the Grand Master, which the knights refused. In 1357, having persuaded the 12-year-old Grand Master that the king was prepared to recognize his sole authority over the Order, the new Grand Master traveled to Seville, where he was quickly and efficiently murdered by the Kings' loyal henchmen.

In 1445, the Order elected Alvaro de Luna, Constable of Castile, but he too was faced with a rival. The alternate Grand Master this time was the heir to the King of Aragon, and the internal feud this time led to a full and bloody war between the knights of Castile and the knights of Aragon. The conflict wiped out almost a fourth of its membership in a few short years, eliminating much of their political control in the process. In 1515, Charles I (also known as the Holy Roman Emperor Charles V) obtained confirmation of the royal administration of the order and was made its Grand Master, thereafter permanently conceding the Grand Master status to the Crown of Castile.

Organization

The Knights of Santiago have a very hierarchical military structure, which led to many of the problems in their later history. Their singular leader, known as the Grand Master, is attended by a council of 13 equally responsible and powerful knights. Each member of the Council of Thirteen (also known as the Trecenezago) is given a great deal of authority within the knightly order. When the Grand Master dies with no clear heir, it is assumed that any and all of the Trecenzago may claim the position if he can persuade, intimidate, or force the others to accept his rule. This leads to numerous power squabbles as the members of the Council of Thirteen position themselves for eventual leadership. The responsibilities of actual military control, supply lines, and battlefield organization for the Knights of Santiago were divided between five Grand Commanders (who might or might not be members of the Trecenezago). These Grand Commanders occupied and controlled all the knights within a kingdom: Castile, León, Montalbán (or Aragón), Portugal, and Gascony.

Because they were outside the military chain of command, the religious members (known as Canons and Canonesses) followed the order of another individual: the Prior. This person was not a member of the Trecenezago or a member of the military chain of command. Only the Grand Master could command the Prior, and, in times of internal strife, the Prior often took control long enough to indoctrinate a new Grand Master.

A Knight of the Order

The Knights of Santiago are flashy, showy individuals who pride themselves on their turnout and their magnificent trappings. Although they do not often have a peacock's elaborate feathers, they are occasionally vain and often insist on the finest of equipment. Their gear may be sparse and they travel light, but what they do carry will always be of the finest quality and the best make.

Most knights of the order are of Castilian descent, their dark hair and eyes marking the background and heritage of their people. They are of noble bloodlines but are unafraid to get their hands dirty – calluses are common even on the most soft-looking knight's hands. They often have scars or other signs of war and battle.

Arms of the Order of Santiago

The Cross of the Order of Santiago is a red Latin cross with flory ends to its three upper arms (in heraldry, this is known as a "cross flory fitchy"). The lower pole is shaped like a sword rather than like the arm of a cross.

Knights of the Order of Santiago wear white robes resembling a monk's habit. The

Shield of the Knights of Santiago

Type: Large Metal Shield
AC Bonus: +3 (+2 base, +1 enchantment)
Armor Check Penalty: 0
Arcane Spell Failure: 5%
Weight: 5 lb

This shield is painted with the formal badge of the Knights of Santiago and has the ability to resist all forms of damage. The shield cannot be injured, even by the most vicious or powerful blow, and the bearer is immune to all damage from fire, acid, and cold.

cross of their order is sewn over the heart, on the left side of the tabard. Masters and other notables may also wear the badge of their order. Those who are empowered to wear it carry it as a cross of the gold and red. It may be suspended from a red ribbon, or it may be sewn onto the left breast.

How Do I Join?

To qualify for membership, candidates of the Knights of Santiago must be of noble birth for at least four generations, but that nobility can be only on his father's side (thus allowing noble-born bastards and those children who have no hope of inheritance from their lineage). Further, their parents must both be baptized into the Christian Faith and be practicing Catholics in good standing. The petitioner must also be a practicing Catholic in good standing and must be willing to serve a four-year tenure as squire to a full knight of the order. At the end of that tenure, the applicant is offered the oaths of service. Generally, only one ceremony admitting new knights is held each year.

Novices were further made to serve as retainers, working in the kitchens and as serving-men or squires to the entire order for six months. During this time, they lived in the Convent of the Order and studied the oaths, the Bible, and the beliefs of the Knights of Santiago. These relatively modest duties could be dispensed with by payment of a sum of money, and some knights who were trying to join the order swiftly would often make a generous contribution to the monastery in order to bypass these obligations. Although the Knights of Santiago were allowed to marry, the wives of knights were carefully chosen and could only be bound in matrimony to a knight with the permission of the Grand Master. These women were asked to provide the same noble proofs as their husbands.

Benefits of Membership

All equipment carried by a member of this order is considered Masterwork quality. The Knights of Santiago always had the finest equipment, and they were never satisfied with second-rate equipment. Characters belonging to the order may purchase Masterwork equipment at standard prices. However, no member of the order would ever allow his equipment to become worn. A Knight of Santiago is always spending. New equipment after each adventure is a must. The best meals, the finest horses, and all the other aspects of the "good life" are necessary for members of this order. It is not about having these things for themselves; it is about maintaining the high honor of being a member of the order. Thus, while these knights can purchase better equipment for the standard price (for it is an honor to equip a knight of this stature), they tend to have less money than others of their rank since they must spend it to keep up appearances.

Chapter 5: Order of Saint James of Compostela

The Order of St. James appeared in Portugal as early as 1172 and was organized originally as a group of noble knights whose duty was to help the first Kings of Portugal drive the Moors out of their territory. The Moors invaded southern Spain as well as Portugal in great numbers, and the Christian kings of those areas were hard-pressed to protect their territories from the invading horde. The order was originally one of Spanish knights, but it quickly gained a political and patriotic role in Portugal, recruiting only those knights of Portuguese stock and background. Soon diverging entirely from its Spanish origins, the Order of St. James of Compostela depended only on the Kings of Portugal and the donation of land and taxes that the knights helped to conquer from the Moors. They were fiscally independent, with their own estates and charterhouse, and they owed their loyalty only to the Portuguese King.

By the middle of the 13th Century, Dom Paio Peres Correia was elected Grand Master of the Order in the Chapter General, beginning a period of great influence within the Portuguese royal government. The order gained a great deal of power over many noble officers, and began to use it ruthlessly in order to further its goals. This swiftly led to severe conflicts between the Portuguese knights and the king, which ended when the Portuguese King exercised his power to revoke the order's taxation benefits and estates, and the knights were forced to rely on Castilian support in order to keep their order alive. Humbled by the experience, the Knights of St. James of Compostela renewed their sovereign vows and gave up political power in order to return to their original goals – to rid Portugal of Moorish invasions.

The Sword of Humility

The Sword of Humility is a +2 Holy greatsword, and conforms to the following stats:

Damage: 2d6 (plus Holy Damage of 2d6)

Crit: 19-20 x2

Range: —

Weight: 10 lbs

Type: Slashing

The Sword of Humility bestows one Negative Level on any evil creature that attempts to wield it. The Negative Level remains as long as the creature holds the weapon and disappears when it is cast aside.

The Sword of Humility is never wielded by the Grand Master of the Order of St. James of Compostela but is always in the hands of one of the lesser knights who proved himself trustworthy and earnest. The weapon responds only to true humility; if there is pride in the wielder's heart, the sword loses all of its bonuses and powers instantly and must be transferred to a new user until the wielder undergoes a rite of penance to cleanse his soul.

History

The Order of St. James of Compostela was founded in Portugal in the 12th Century. Its name comes from an original (and somewhat ironic) dedication to the national patron of Spain, St. James the Greater, whose grave was discovered in northern Spain in the Ninth Century. Inspired by this symbol of holy favor, the Christians drove back the Moorish and Muslim influences that invaded Spain, and freed the kingdom for Christian rule. The city of Compostela in Galicia is the clear center of devotion to this apostle and calls many thousands of pilgrims each year from both Spain and Portugal.

During the period of this order's inception, the royal dynasty of Spain was divided and feuding. Two separate claimants to the throne each demanded that they were the rightful King, and neither would abdicate their claim for the benefit of the nation. The Knights of Santiago involved themselves seriously in these feuds, leaving many of the poorer and less famous knightly orders to tend to the people of Spain and Portugal. The Knights of St. James of Compostela were among these lesser groups.

Unlike the contemporary orders of Calatrava and Alcántara, which followed the severe dictates of the Benedictines, the Knights of St. James adopted the milder dictates of the

The Sword of Humility (cont'd)

While being brandished by someone of humble heart and good motive, the Sword of Humility projects an aura in a 20-foot radius that blocks all incoming mind-affecting spells and gives all those within the range of effect the Thief ability, Evasion. Further, when wielded in defense of Spain or a Spanish noble, the sword begins to "sing." All those in audible range of the weapon must make a Will Save each round at a DC of 17 or fall to their knees and refuse to fight against the sword's wielder. If this occurs, the affected individuals are so overwhelmed by the knowledge of their place in the world that they can no longer fight.

The Sword of Humility can never be used against truly innocent creatures or against faithful members of the Order of St. James of Compostela (whatever their alignment may be). In these instances, the sword simply does no damage and will never show its supernatural abilities.

Canons of St. Augustine, allowing them to be more open and available to the poor and the sick. The mildness of this rule furthered the rapid spread of the order, and their numbers quickly eclipsed those of much older orders in Spain and Portugal. The first Bull of confirmation, that of Alexander III, already enumerated a large number of endowments. The Knights of St. James, although their order was still small, offered their services for the protection of pilgrims to the shrine of St. James and the hospices on the roads leading to Compostela. They were frequently seen on these highways as well as along the border to the Moorish lands and took their duties very seriously. In the absence of the "larger orders," the Knights of St. James were a godsend.

The Order of St. James was recognized as a fully qualified religious knighthood by Pope Alexander III, who secured them all the privileges and exemptions of other monastic orders. Once they received this official blessing, they grew at an even greater rate, and expanded fully into Portugal. They made their capital within the Portuguese boundaries, and invited several members of the Portuguese royal family to join their order of knighthood. Their wealth grew as well, and the Knights of St. James began relying heavily on the taxes and moneys of those lands to further their order. At the height of their political control, they maintained possessions in Portugal, France, Italy, Hungary, and even Palestine.

They assisted in driving out the Muslims, doing battle with them sometimes separately, sometimes with the royal armies. Finally, they took part in the maritime expeditions against the Muslims. One of their most powerful Grand Masters died under questionable circumstances, leading to a radical shift in the order's prominence. He had had 39 successors, some of which were close to the line of Portuguese Kings. Internally, the Knights of St. James began to lose their solidarity and the political control they had enjoyed for nearly three generations. Eventually, the Portuguese King exercised his power to revoke the order's taxation benefits and estates. The Order of St. James found itself impoverished, its lands seized or cut off, and its power over the throne destroyed forever. At this point, the knights had no choice but to turn back to the Knights of Santiago and seek their origins within Castile – a punishing blow for the once-proud and independent Portuguese knighthood.

Pilgrimage

In 813 AD, the burial site of St. James the Great, the first cousin (sometimes called the brother) of Jesus and one of His most favored apostles, was discovered in Spain, near the small city of Compostela. This site was marked by God, according to nearby viewers, who shone a strange, unnatural light from the sky in order to lead the faithful to the spot where the saint was buried. Within the small tomb were found numerous relics and the bones of the saint himself. It was quickly sealed again, and became a site for thousands of pilgrims in the Middle Ages, who traveled hundreds of miles to prove their loyalty to God and in order to beg the saint for intervention or for healing.

The discovery of the holy saint and his relics provided a rallying point for Christian Spain, and electrified the Christian beliefs of the country and the peasants. The site was a national favorite, a patron saint to the Spanish, who inducted its occupant to the highest calling they could imagine: they made St. James the patron saint of Spain.

The site became well-traveled, and many bandits took to haunting the roadside hoping to find wealthy pilgrims to attack. The tomb itself was in a dangerous location, confined to a narrow strip at the north of the Iberian Peninsula, most of which was occupied by Moors. In order to protect the Christian Faithful, Kind Alfonso II of Asturias built a large and sturdy church over the stone tomb, sheltering those who would come to visit the resting place of the saint. The city was dominated by the great church, its labyrinthine streets leading toward the central structure from every direction. The Church of St. James towered two stories above the central plaza, with towers that soared into the sky. The interior was decoratively carved with images from St. James' life, and pilgrims would often bend to touch the hearth of the church with their hands before they entered.

Organization

The Order of St. James of Compostela was fairly loosely structured, a throwback to its origins as an order of peasant-knights. When it reached prominence, it was structured much like a feudal system, with a Grand Master and numerous serjeants that served and followed his rule. Clear succession was handled by the serjeant with the most years of service, or who had been specifically chosen as heir by the Grand Master prior to his death.

A Knight of the Order

A common knight of the Order of St. James was a Portuguese man, with a simply-trapped hose and common garb. He might have worn the robes of his order, but, in general, such things were used only for formal occasions. The knight traveled in his own clothing, wearing only the badge of the order around his neck. In later years, when the order gained significant prominence and wealth, the knights dressed

Armor of the Knights of St. James of Compostela

Type: Full Plate Armor

AC Bonus: +9 (+8 base, +1 enchantment)

Max Dex Bonus: +3

Armor Check Penalty: -3

Arcane Spell Failure: 25%

Speed: 20 feet

Weight: 30 lbs

This magical suit of armor was given to the Knights of St. James of Compostela after their fall from grace. It was a blessing from the pope, restoring their charge and asking them to go forth in humility, remembering that pride was their downfall. The armor is therefore only worn by a youthful and earnest member of the order rather than a prestigious Master or Grand Master, and it is only used when there is great need. It is considered one of the most sacred relics of the order and is protected and cared for with almost religious respect.

Armor of the Knights of St. James of Compostela (cont'd)

The armor is a pale gold in color, forged from the finest steel and inlaid with green and red tracings across the shoulders and breastplate. The front plate of the armor is emblazoned with the red cross of the Knights of St. James of Compostela and seems to be forged as one with the steel of the armor rather than enameled upon the breast. The armor itself seems almost flimsy, as if it was made only for courtly appearances and not for protection, but it is as stalwart and sturdy a piece of armor as any other in the world. While wearing it, the bearer cannot be injured by any ranged attacks, be they magical or physical. All such attacks simply stop five feet from the wearer, falling to ash without causing any harm.

more opulently and traveled with large entourages of squires. After their fall from grace, they reverted to their common garb and simple accoutrements, claiming that humility was God's gift to their order.

Arms of the Order of St. James

The Order of St. James is known by the badge that its knights wear. They do not tend to wear formal robes, but will always have the badge of on a ribbon around their necks. This badge is shaped in the sign of a St. James' Cross, fleury, and enameled red with edges of gold. The cross is displayed within two palm branches enameled green and rests upon a silver scroll inscribed, *"Sciencias, Letras e Artes,"* (sciences, letters, and arts) in letters of gold. Their symbol, when painted or sewn onto a formal robe, is a red fleury cross which reflects their connection with the pilgrimage of St. James.

Those who are Masters of the Order may also wear a multi-pointed star in gold (in silver for Commanders), with asymmetrical rays, charged in the center, upon a field of silver. Inside the star is a small representation of the Badge of the Order.

In later years, the Portuguese knights began to use a very specific symbol to show their complete independence from their parent order in Spain. This badge used a purple sword-like cross rather than the red fleury sign of St. James. The Ribbon is plain lilac to distinguish itself from the Order of Christ.

Benefits of Membership

The Knights of St. James all receive a +1 Class Bonus to all attacks made against Moors. This reflects their fanatical devotion to driving the Moors out of

Shield of the Knights of St. James of Compostela

Type: Large Metal Shield

AC Bonus: +3 (+2 base, +1 enchantment)

Armor Check Penalty: 0

Arcane Spell Failure: 5%

Weight: 5 lbs

This shield is painted with the formal badge of the Knights of St. John of Compostela but otherwise appears to be no more than a common steel shield. It is somewhat battered and dented but still sturdy, and, although the paint is chipped, it seems to radiate an aura of safety and strength. The bearer receives an additional +4 to all Bull Rush attempts while using this shield.

Spain and Portugal and defending pilgrims who come to worship at the Tomb of St. James. ***The knights also gain a +4 Class Bonus to all Heal checks as a result of their work with the sick, the poor, and pilgrims.***

Chapter 6: The Knights of Calatrava

This famous and well-respected order of knights began as the military wing of the Knights Hospitaller but soon became an independent group which owed no fealty to any other order. When they separated from the Knights Hospitaller in order to tend to Spain, they were the first order of knights in that country. They are the oldest military order in Spain, and much respected for their loyalty and their duty to the Spanish Crown.

The original capital of the order is the fortress of Calatrava la Vieja in central Spain. Founded by the Spaniards as a defense against the Moors, the order led every battle against the Muslims and considered itself the "Bastion of Christian Faith." In 1213, the King of León, Alfonso IX, gave the Knights of Calatrava a massive keep in the city of Alcántara. The knights accepted and moved their capital, changing the name of the order to "Order of Alcántara." They continued as strong and fierce warriors against the Muslims and actively sought to hunt down and destroy the enemies of Christianity rather than simply waiting and defending against their invasions. The Knights of Calatrava were fanatics and extremists, eager to see their blades bloodied by war against all heretical faiths.

History

The Knights of Calatrava took an approach opposite of many other orders. Rather than a group of knights seeking to become patriots of the faith, those who had been monks sought to become knights, learning martial skills in order to defend and serve the Spanish crown. They fought to sustain their piety despite the deaths of thousands of Christians at Muslim hands, and, consequently, they resolved that, in order to tend the flock, they would be forced to kill the wolves. Thus, these simple monks took up arms. Eventually, they became the foundation of the largest and most dedicated order of fanatic knights in all of Christendom. These were strong and impetuous monks, who by their nature did nothing by halves. They described their need to fight as a willingness to struggle in order to reach the Gates of Heaven; in order to do so, they seized earthly strongholds and routed Muslim defenders with fanatic intent.

Calatrava is the Arabic name of a castle recovered from the Muslims in 1147. Situated on the extreme southern borders of Castile, it was a tremendous coup to take the fortress, and the Christian Spanish did not know if they could hold it against the constant invasions and sieges of the Muslim powers. After a vain attempt to defend Calatrava, the Knights Templar abandoned it, claiming that it could not be held against the infidels.

Raymond, Abbot of the Cistercian monastery of Fitero, offered himself and his men, who were all eager for battle and willing to lay their lives on the line for their faith. The push for this idea allegedly came from a simple monk within the order, one who was a knight retired into the monastery but who trained his fellow brothers with sword and shield in his spare time. The King, unaccustomed to controlling military matters, was inspired with the idea of allowing the faithful brothers of the abbey to defend Calatrava. Three years after they moved

The Sword of Devotion

The Sword of Devotion is a +3 Holy greatsword and conforms to the following stats:

Damage: 2d6 (plus Holy Damage of 3d6)

Crit: 18-20 x2

Range: —

Weight: 10 lbs

Type: Slashing

The Sword of Devotion bestows one Negative Level on any Evil creature that attempts to wield it. The Negative Level remains as long as the creature holds the weapon and vanishes when the weapon is no longer wielded.

The Sword of Devotion is a fanatic's weapon, created to do as much damage to the enemy as possible with little thought for defense or protection. Those who wield it may exchange AC for damage bonuses at a 1-for-1 ratio (therefore, dropping AC by three points will increase damage by three points). Further, the user's Threatened Area extends to 10 feet away from him or her rather than the usual five feet as the sword's overwhelming fanaticism and tenaciousness grants him or her an amazing amount of speed and stamina.

into the keep, holding it firm against all Muslim invaders, they received the name and knighthood of their order and joined the Knights Hospitallers as a branch of their highly-regarded order.

Once they proved that they could successfully keep the castle safe against all external threats, the eager monks asked to take the offensive against the Moors. At the same time, those monks who did not enjoy the idea of permanently becoming a militant order left the keep. Only the knights, their Grand Commander Velasquez, and a few chaplains, remained in Calatrava.

The Knights of Calatrava determined a rule of behavior that all members would follow. This rule, modeled upon the Cistercian customs they followed as monks, imposed upon the knights certain monastic obligations. They were asked to take the three religious vows (poverty, chastity, and obedience), as well as following the rules of silence in the refectory, dormitory, and oratory. They were required to fast in abstinence during the day four days a week, and keep holy several fast days during the year.

The first military services of the Knights of Calatrava were brilliant, and, in return for the great services they had rendered, they received from the King of Castile new grants of land, which formed their first commanderies. But these successes were followed by a series of misfortunes due to the consequent rivalry of the Spanish throne. To the south, the Moors of Spain continued in their attacks against the Spanish and Portuguese Christians. They called upon the African Moors and brought redoubled troops into the Spanish borders in order to crush the resistance of the Spanish knights and were successful. The battle of Alarcos was devastating to the Christians, and the fanatic Calatravan knights were overpowered. The keep was taken, and Calatrava was lost.

The scattered remains of the order found shelter in Cirvelos and began to repair their losses by recruiting and inducting a large number of new knights. Yet still, their efforts to unseat the Moors from Calatrava and the southern border of Spain failed miserably, and the order was beaten back once more. At last, Pope Innocent III turned his eyes to the desperate struggle. He called upon foreign crusaders, asking the knights of Aragon, León, France, and England to hurry to the side of the Knights of Calatrava and aid them in displacing the Moorish invaders. The first event in this holy war, now a European one, was the Reconquista – the re-conquest of Calatrava.

Following the Spanish victories, the Knights Hospitaller, Knights Templar, and the Knights of Calatrava forged an alliance and drove deeply into the heart of Muslim territories. The Moors were beaten back, and this began the decline of Muslim domination in Western Europe. Working together and aiding one another, the knightly orders marked the climax of chivalry and the greatest deeds of their time. During this brief period, the Spanish King Ferdinand (known later as Ferdinand the Saint) dealt a mortal blow to the Muslim power. He used the power of the knights, led by the fanatic and bloodthirsty Knights of Calatrava, to seize the Muslim capital city of Cordova. That victory was soon followed by the surrender of Murcia, Jaen, and Seville.

Calatrava, with its abundant resources of men and wealth, had by this time become a great power within Spain. It seceded peacefully from the Knights Hospitaller, becoming a fully independent order, and it gained even more lands and castles scattered along the borders of Castile. The Knights of Calatrava were seen as the most powerful knights in Spain and possibly the strongest order in Christendom. Yet still, they fought to be allowed to further beat back the Moors from the borders of Spain. The order could field 1200 to 2000 knights easily – a very considerable force in the Middle Ages. Moreover, as a holy order of knights, they enjoyed autonomy, acknowledging only spiritual superiors such as the Cardinal of Spain and the pope. Yet, internally, the order began to suffer internal rivalries. Their Grand Masters were constantly dying off in battle, and often the line of succession was unclear. The Knights of Calatrava were not immune to the intrigues of the Spanish court either, and those political rivalries began to affect the knights of the order. After the 14th Century, the rigorous discipline and fervent observance of the order's earlier times had given place to a spirit of intrigue and ambition.

With the accession of Pedro the Cruel as king of Spain, the order began to deeply suffer for its political ambitions. Three Grand Commanders in succession were put to death by the Spanish Crown: the first of these was beheaded; the second was murdered in the royal palace by the king's own treacherous hand; and the third fell into disgrace and died in prison. The order fell into political disgrace, seen now openly as bloodthirsty fanatics. The knights broke into rival factions, and their internal

The Sword of Devotion (cont'd)

Targets affected by the Sword of Devotion suffer wounds that can only be healed through magical aid. These cuts will not seal normally, nor will time cause them to get better. Those who suffer these injuries and have no readily available magical healing suffer the curse of open wounds in the Middle Ages – their wounds quickly turn diseased. Every day that the wounds are not healed at least partially, the afflicted character must make a Fortitude Save to prevent infection. The DC for this Saving Throw beings at 12 and rises by one every day. Those whose wounds become infected suffer 1d3 points of Constitution Damage per day. Only a Remove Disease spell or amputation of the infected limb can save the victim under these circumstances.

The Sword of Devotion can never be used against faithful members of the Knights of Calatrava or against a member of the direct bloodline of the Kings of Spain or Portugal (whatever their Alignment may be). In these instances, the sword simply does no damage no matter how brutally wielded.

Armor of the Knights of Calatrava

Type: Full Plate Armor

AC Bonus: +11 (+8 base, +3 enchantment)

Max Dex Bonus: +3

Armor Check Penalty: -3

Arcane Spell Failure: 25%

Speed: 20 feet

Weight: 30 lbs

The Knights of Calatrava are known for their fanaticism and their brutal strength, and the armor they bear is made to withstand both the attacks of their enemies and the rage of their own fervor. Their most famous suit of armor was forged by the first Grand Master of the order and has been remade on several occasions (since those who wear the armor do not always survive their own battle-rage and religious frenzies). Although the armor is considered one of the most sacred relics of the order, it is cared for by monks and chaplains rather than by the knights themselves. This prevents any untoward use of the armor and keeps the battle-rage chained within it from affecting any would-be heroes of the order.

The armor is blue-grey in color and is inlaid with scarlet and white tracings across the shoulders and wrists. The front plate is emblazoned with the scarlet badge of the order, and the helm is covered with a pure white plume. When in battle, the individual wearing it may call upon a Barbaric Rage. This is identical to the Barbarian Rage Class Feature. The suit can be triggered to grant this ability twice per day.

structure began to fragment. Several times, it seemed as if a Grand Commander would rise to lead them back into prominence only to see him cut down by treachery or circumstance.

Yet the order was still wealthy since its internal strife did little to reduce the fine estates and lands that were held independent of taxation. The Knights of Calatrava owned more than 50 keeps and commanderies, with 16 full monastic priories in total. The sum of taxable estates included 64 villages with a population of 200,000 and an annual income which is estimated at 50,000 ducats. The revolving kings of Spain coveted these riches, and watched while the order's fluctuating leadership allowed these wealthy estates and holdings to lay fallow, untaxed and simply providing money to be squandered without any means for the knights to indulge. If there were a war or if the borders of Spain were once more threatened by the Moorish enemy, the Knights of Calatrava were capable of spending three times the ducats that the royal throne could muster to defeat the enemy.

But for a short period, the knights seemed as if they might regain their footing. Though the kings of Spain struggled to steal their lands and moneys, a new and unified Grand Commander rose within the order. This man was Lopez de Padilla, the last of the 27 independent grand masters of Calatrava. While he ruled that order, there was peace and the knights lived in prosperity once more. They began to turn their eyes again toward the destruction of the Moorish lands on the Spanish borders. During the conquest of the last Moorish stronghold – the Kingdom of Granada – the Knights of Calatrava were inexhaustible. Their final victory, the fall of Granada, also signaled the fall of their order (see the Avalanche Press board game, GRANADA: THE FALL OF MOSLEM SPAIN, for more on this struggle). Shortly after they defeated the Moors, the order was disbanded by the King of Spain.

Organization

The teachings of the Cistercian Saint Bernard of Clairvaux taught the Knights of Calatrava how to live within an ideal of religious-military life. Their prior background as monks further organized the order, structuring them more like a priorship or a Catholic monastery rather than as a military order.

The order possessed a strong sense of unity, brotherhood, discipline, and purpose. Each commanderie was organized around a small group (usually 7 to 10) of knight-brothers, who ruled jointly. These knight-brothers were overseen by an advisor, the commanderie's chaplain, who owed obedience only to the Grand Commander at Calatrava.

The head of the Order was the Grand Commander, his deputy the Grand Commander of Alcañices (or of Aragón). Other important offices within the order were the Clavero, or keeper of the keys; the Alférez (Standard-Bearer); and the High Commander of Almodovar.

Shield of the Knights of Calatrava

Type: Large Metal Shield

AC Bonus: +5 (+2 base, +3 enchantment)

Armor Check Penalty: 0

Arcane Spell Failure: 5%

Weight: 5 lbs

While most of the Knights of Calatrava do not carry a shield (the most popular weapon among the order is a great sword), the order was presented with this singular item by the Kings of Spain upon their seizure of the Calatrava fortress and the founding of their order. The shield is enameled with the scarlet cross of their order, and gives its bearer a free attempt to disarm one opponent per round without expending an Attack Action.

A Knight of the Order

A common knight of the Order of Calatrava is a fierce fighting man, someone with many scars and well-used armor. While he often keeps the symbol of the order present on his gear, he is always prepared for instant battle and does not use ornate or purely decorative robes or accoutrements. These are hard, stern men with little on their minds other than the quest to rid the world of Moors and Muslims, and they are unrelenting in their pursuit of that goal.

Arms of the Knights of Calatrava

After it became an independent order of knights, the Order of Calatrava began to wear its own habit, a distinguishable costume that set its members apart in court and on the battlefield. They used their badge and heraldry in many different ways, blazoning it on tunic, armor, shield, and flag in order to make themselves distinct to their hated enemy and to their companions on the battlefield. Their standard ritual dress included a simple white mantle with a scarlet cross on the left shoulder. The acknowledged symbol of their order is a scarlet cross on a white or blue field.

How Do I Join?

The Knights of Calatrava are a fanatic military organization feared for their courage, dedication, and strong will to see their goals achieved. They do not accept any members who are not willing to risk their lives on the field of battle against the Moors; they further do not accept non-Christians or those who are already injured or impaired and cannot fight.

As monks, the Knights of Calatrava actively seek out religious individuals to fill their ranks. Those born in Spain are preferred, but they do not discriminate against other faithful individuals willing to fight for the cause. Although they do have lineage requirements (one parent must be noble), the Knights of Calatrava are among the most likely to ignore a questionable parentage if the individual in question would strongly benefit the knighthood's goals.

After an individual expresses an interest in joining the Order of Calatrava, he must undergo rigorous religious and martial training as a squire to a brother of the order, even if the petitioner is already knighted. This term of service dedicates the new member to the knighthood and teaches him the difficult life of the Knight of Calatrava. He is expected to carry out his duties on the battlefield even if that means a martyr's death. Nothing less is tolerated, and those who are not fanatical enough or not capable are turned away.

Benefits of Membership

All members of the Knights of Calatrava receive a +1 Class Bonus to all attacks against Moors and Muslims. The knights are fanatical in their desire to wipe these peoples from the face of the Earth, and this bonus is representative of that zeal.

Once per day, members of the order can also cast the Divine Spell, Divine Favor. This is an innate ability more than a spell (since magic would be seen as heretical), but the effects are the same. God imbues these knights with extra power to smite their enemies.

Chapter 7: Order of the Knights of Christ

The Aragonese Order known as the Knights of Christ originates from the Portuguese priory of Knights Templar, which simply changed its name when that order was suppressed by Pope Clement. These knights were, in their own fashion, rebels and political revolutionaries against an oppressive spiritual government. For the most part, they were successful – afraid of losing the political support and wealth that the Knightly Order offered to its allies, the body of Aragon nobility simply accepted the order's new name and apparent independence – and it became courtly practice not to notice that this "new" order just happened to be exactly the same as the old.

When the Knights Templar were dissolved, King Jaime II of Aragon created a new order of knights from the Aragonese branch of Templars. This order spread throughout Portugal and into Spain, and those knights still loyal to the Templar cause swiftly joined forces with the "new" order. Supposedly, the primary mission of this order was to defend the coast of Valencia against Moorish pirates – something that the Knights Templar (now unified with the remnants of the Knights Hospitallers as the Knights of Rhodes) were already achieving.

Their decisive impact on Moorish conquest was only balanced by their constant relationship with Cathar beliefs, and eventually the Inquisition brought in most of the Knights of Christ as Cathar heretics and blasphemers. This led to the order's eventual fall from prominence, and they were disbanded in disgrace.

History

The Knights of Christ were established in the Kingdom of Aragon to take the place of the Order of the Knights Templar, which was disbanded and reformed with the Knights Hospitaller after 1312.

In the beginning, the Knights Templar were well received in Aragon and Castile. Berenger III, Count of Barcelona, proclaimed in his will that he wished to die in the habit of a Templar. King Alfonso I, having no direct heir, bequeathed his dominions to be divided among the Templars, the Hospitallers, and

The Sword of Honor

The Sword of Honor is a +2 Holy longsword, and conforms to the following stats:

Damage: 1d8 (plus Holy Damage of 1d6)

Crit: 19-20 x2

Range: —

Weight: 3 lb

Type: Slashing

The Sword of Honor bestows one Negative Level on any Evil creature that attempts to wield it, which remains as long as the creature holds the weapon and disappears when the weapon is dropped.

The Sword of Honor is a weapon of prophecy. It is said that one day it will be used against the returned Christ and will break its blade rather than cause him injury. In this way, the Knights of Christ will know their Lord on High. The Sword of Honor will not abide an oath-breaker or a liar. If its wielder ever commits either sin, the sword's blade will become bloody and never again be clean. It will never cause harm to its wielder's enemies in this state. Once it has become ruined in this fashion, the only hope is for a new owner to take it up, washing the blood clean and pledging his or her honor to the sword.

the Canons of the Holy Sepulcher. That request was denied by his advisors after his death since it would effectively have given away the entire kingdom to the Church.

Although the Aragonese branch of the order was pronounced innocent at the famous trial of the Templars, Clement V's Bull of suppression was applied to them in spite of the protests of King Jaime II. By way of compensation, however, this monarch obtained from Pope John XXII authority to dispose of the possessions of the Templars in his Kingdom of Valencia in favor of a military order not essentially differing from that of the Templars charged with the defense of his frontier against the Moors and the pirates. The first of the 14 Grand Masters who ruled the Knights of Christ until the office was united with the Crown by Philip II in 1587 was Guillermo d'Eril. The much smaller Order of the Knights of Christ was territorially limited to the Kingdom of Aragon (which included Valencia).

With the approval of antipope Benedict XIII it was amalgamated with the Aragonese Order of Montesa and gained a significant amount of power and prestige in Aragon. For a time, it

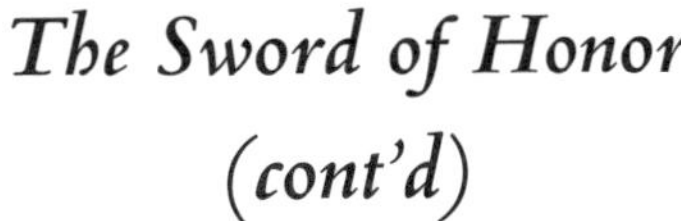

The Sword of Honor (cont'd)

The wielder of the Sword of Honor may make a Full Attack without suffering any penalties to his or her movement for the round. Further, anyone willingly swearing an oath on the sword's blade will find himself or herself completely unable to break that oath under any circumstances, even if it means death to attempt to complete the promise.

The Sword of Honor can never be used against faithful members of the Knights of Christ (whatever their Alignment may be). If the sword is wielded against a member of this order, it will immediately disarm itself from the current wielder, hurling itself 15 feet in a random direction.

Armor of the Knights of Christ

Type: Full Plate Armor

AC Bonus: +10 (+8 base, +2 enchantment)

Max Dex Bonus: +3

Armor Check Penalty: -3

Arcane Spell Failure: 25%

Speed: 20 feet

Weight: 30 lbs

The Order of the Knights of Christ are deeply entwined with the mystical Christian group known as the Cathars, who most certainly crafted this suit of plate mail for the order's Grand Master. The armor remains, all but forgotten, in the deepest catacombs of their headquarters. Since the Cathars fell from grace and were hunted by the Church as heretics, the Knights of Christ chose to hide their connection to these ancient allies. The armor is almost never worn, and few within the order even know of its existence.

The armor is red, forged to appear as though the steel of the plates was soaked in or stained with blood. The arms, shoulders, and legs are inlaid with silvery tracings across the shoulders and breastplate. The front plate is emblazoned with a pale white cross denoting the bearer as a member of the Knights of Christ. While wearing the armor, the knight has the ability to cast Dimension Door up to five times a day. The wearer may bring up to two others along on this travel so long as they are also Knights of Christ.

seemed as if the Knights of Christ needed only a few years and they would restore the authority of the Knights Templar, but that was never to occur. The pauper prince of Aragon was unable to assure a sufficient endowment for the support of his knights, and so the order began to falter. The knights were in such trouble of falling to complete pauperism that they were no longer asked to take a vow of poverty. Instead, they simply swore obedience and chastity, but, owing to this lack of resources, the order did not survive.

Purpose & Organization

The purpose of the Knights of Christ was primarily to "get around" the papal edicts that ended the Knights Templar. Although they were essentially a separate order, the Knights of Christ maintained the militant stance and honorable decorum known of their original order, and their stance against Islam did not alter at all. They did occasionally engage in sea battles (but not as often as the Knights of Rhodes, the official successors to the Knights Templar), and they did stand against any and all Moorish or Muslim invasions of Spain, Aragon, or Portugal. They were a quiet order, and a poor one, but they stood stalwart in their ideals and goals.

A Knight of the Order

The Knights of Christ were the poorest order in existence, living off the last remnants of the Knights Templar and the King's grace within Aragon. Their clothing was dull, and often patched, and whatever armor or weapons they possessed were always very plain and serviceable. In some areas, a band of traveling Knights of Christ might be mistaken for a group of peasants or bandits. Before they were ordered to join with the Knights of Montesa, the Knights of Christ were almost entirely older, seasoned knights too set in their ways to change when the Knights Templar were "disbanded" by the pope. Only after they merged with the Knights of Montesa were there any young knights within the order again.

Arms of the Knights of Christ

This Order had a well-known symbol, patently its own despite the group's origins within the Knights Templar. The Knights of the Order of Christ bore a red on white hollow cross, a symbol that outlived the Order itself and began to be used by many nobles of Aragon and Portuguese descent. Flags of the order had this cross over a number of backgrounds, most frequently using white, green, and white/green gyronny, with the latter said to be the most "correct."

The ribbon or badge of the Order of Montesa is identical to that of Calatrava but forged in black rather than gold. The badge is ensigned with a plain red Greek cross suspended from a red ribbon or sewn on the left breast.

Benefits of Membership

Members of the Knights of Christ gain a +2 Class Bonus to all Will Saving Throws. They also gain a +2 Faith Bonus to their AC against all Muslims.

Shield of the Knights of Christ

Type: Large Metal Shield

AC Bonus: +2

Armor Check Penalty: 0

Arcane Spell Failure: 5%

Weight: 5 lbs

Also created by the Cathars as a companion piece to the Armor of the Knights of Christ, this shield is lost and may in fact have been destroyed. It was last seen more than 100 years ago, and its bearer never returned from his mission into the heartland of the Moors. The shield is painted with the formal badge of the Knights of Christ and enables its bearer to turn Muslim priests as if they were undead of equivalent level. Though, it was likely destroyed by the heretics for this powerful ability, it is possible that, somewhere deep in the heart of Moorish territory, it still exists.

Chapter 8: Teutonic Knights

The Knights of the Teutonic Order were members of an elite German brotherhood. Raised to be knights from birth (many of whom were actually given to the temple at an early age so that they could be trained), these knights fought in the Northern Crusade of 1320. They dominated northern Europe in the same manner that the Knights of Calatrava held Spain or the Knights Templar possessed the Holy Land. Over the years, the Teutonic Order of Knights spawned several smaller orders – Brethren of the Sword, Order of Dobrin (in Lithuania) and the Dark Order, all of whom outlived their parent guild.

The Teutonic Order was formally known as the *hospitale sancte Marie Theutonicorum Jerosolimitanum* – the Hospital of St. Mary of the Germans of Jerusalem – or in some of the northern countries, *der orden des Düschen huses* – the order of the German houses. Along with the Templars and the Hospitallers, it was one of the three major knightly and military orders that originated and evolved during the 12th and 13th Centuries.

The Sword of Purity

The Sword of Purity is a +4 Holy longsword, and conforms to the following stats:

Damage: 1d8 (plus Holy Damage of 2d6)

Crit: 19-20 x2

Range: —

Weight: 3 lb

Type: Slashing

The Sword of Purity bestows two Negative Levels on any Evil creature that attempts to wield it. It also bestows one Negative Level on any non-German individual that attempts to wield it. The Negative Levels remain as long as the weapon is held and disappear when it is discarded.

According to legend, the Sword of Purity was created of the Virgin Mary's tears upon the rocks of Germany. Its blade is dark grey, almost the color of iron, but it is easily as hard as steel. It has the ability to cut through any material, no matter how strong or how well enchanted. The sword ignores all AC bonuses granted by armor, tough hide, or other outward covering.

The Sword of Loyalty can never be used against individuals of noble German stock or against faithful members of the Teutonic Knights (whatever their Alignment may be). In these instances, the sword howls in rage, and all damage which would have been given by the blow is suffered by the wielder instead.

The Teutonic order was governed by the Church as a cloister of monks but was also given many allowances usually reserved for the upper echelons of noble society. For most purposes, the Teutonic Order was completely separate from the dictates of temporal government, relegating themselves to the leadership of spiritual entities and was answerable only to the pope. They did have some feudal responsibilities as dictated by circumstances of place and time, particularly, in managing and tending their lands and estates and in response to a declaration of war. These knights rarely left the northern European continent and were typically found in meditation and study rather than at war. As with other knightly orders, the members of the Teutonic Order took vows of poverty, chastity, and obedience upon attaining knighthood.

History

According to tradition, early in the 12th Century a wealthy German couple built a hospital in Jerusalem at their own expense to care for poor and sick pilgrims who spoke German. From their dedication, the knightly order sprang, continuing their tradition and carrying their piety and mercy back into northern Europe.

The German hospitals in the Holy Land affiliated themselves with the Hospital of St. John and observed the rules and oaths of St. Augustine. They were protected by the Knights Hospitallers, and the Teutonic Knights were not yet organized. After Saladin's conquest of Jerusalem in 1187, the German hospital was destroyed and no longer kept. There is no indication that the German hospital ever had a military mission.

During the siege of Acre during the Third Crusade, German knights created a field hospital for soldiers. This hospital was far more a make-shift encampment than a standard inn-style hospice, using ship sails for cover and boiling water in helmets to treat wounds. Pope Clement III (1187-1191) approved the Teutonic Order and blessed their efforts on February 6, 1191 when the order was given the name, "Hospital of St. Mary of the Germans in Jerusalem." The name is the only connection with the earlier German hospital and was soon lost thereafter in the creation and organization of the same group, now known as the Teutonic Knights.

Official recognition of the Teutonic Knights as a separate order of knighthood authorized by the Catholic Church came in February of 1199, by Pope Innocent III. A historian of the time describes the building constructed to be their main chapel in this fashion:

When you go down this street, next to the gate which leads to the Temple, to the right there is a small passage lined with columns, and in this street there are a hostel and a church which were recently built in honor of St. Mary, and this is called "the German building." Anyone who speaks any other language can barely receive a blessing.

Indeed, the Teutonic Knights were very proud of their racial and territorial origins, and believed that their purity of lineage and strength of purpose elevated them above the southern orders of knighthood. Yet, still, they were a hospitaller order, not a militant one, and their goals were simply to tend the needy and care for German pilgrims and citizens within the Holy Land.

On March 5, 1198, the Teutonic Knights were changed forever. After serving in battle to defend Jerusalem, the knights re-forged their purpose, becoming an aggressive militant order rather than simply a passive care-giving one. The patriarch and King of Jerusalem watched from the vanguard of the crusading army and afterwards formally inducted the Teutonic Knights as a military order. A Bull from Pope Innocent III (1198-1216) dated February 19, 1199 confirmed the event and specified the Order would care for the sick and defend the northern Christians within and without the Holy Land. It would conduct all other business by following the Templar rule and members at war would wear the Temple's distinctive white cloak. Their arms, a dark black cross on white rather than the red cross of the Templars, would differentiate the Teutonic Order from the Knights of the Temple.

From the outset, the possessions and wealth of the Teutonic Order grew astoundingly fast and its numbers skyrocketed. Their Grand Masters were on good terms with the stable government of the Holy Roman Empire, and the Teutonic Order gained many favors. Between 1215 and 1300, several commanderies were founded each year, usually through gifts. The order grew, especially in the Holy Roman Empire and the lands to the north.

The Teutonic Order held territory in Greece, Hungary, and Prussia as well as the Holy Roman Empire, and fulfilled their purposes with an iron hand. Often, secular rulers would ask the Teutonic Knights to perform military duties on their behalf, acting as lawgivers and military. Some countries routinely provided fiefs to the Teutonic Knights in return for military service. Eventually, the Teutonic Order became too strong in many of those countries (the difficulties of using a group as law-keepers is that they are eventually seen as the makers of the law). The Hungarian King Andrew II (1205-1235) expelled the Order in 1225 when it became so

Influence by Means Other than Money

While the German Order did not equal the vast wealth and possessions of the Knights Templar and the Knights Hospitaller, it was certainly the only other order to rival them in international influence and activity. The power of the Teutonic Knights was greater, perhaps, because they did not need to financially blackmail their allies in order to gain support. They were seen as noble heroes, justified in their requests, and most of the leaders of northern Europe supported and upheld their power willingly. They maintained a position that most other knighthoods envied for several hundred years.

Armor of the Teutonic Knights

Type: Full Plate Armor

AC Bonus: +12 (+8 base, +4 enchantment)

Max Dex Bonus: +3

Armor Check Penalty: -3

Arcane Spell Failure: 25%

Speed: 20 feet

Weight: 30 lbs

Created long ago by a master smith of the Holy Roman Empire, this magnificent suit of plate mail is known to be one of the strongest artifacts in the world. Legends say that nothing can dent or scratch it and that any knight who wears it has the eye of God upon him during battle. No Teutonic Knight wearing the armor ever fell in combat.

Although a knight wearing this armor is virtually impervious to bladed attacks, he can be brought down by archery or other ranged weapons. The knight takes no damage from melee weapons or attacks, but double damage from any attack launched at range. Magic is treated as normal and is not affected by this armor's capabilities.

The armor is jet black, reflecting not an ounce of sunlight upon its darkened surface. There are no inlays or other frivolous artistic designs upon the armor, and it appears somber and cold. The blazon of the Knights Templar, a white cross, is enameled upon the twin shoulder plates of the armor and again on the cloak worn with the plate mail.

strong that it threatened his rule.

In 1230, the Order's Grand Master was named prince of the Holy Roman Empire and given the same privileges as the Templars and Hospitallers by Pope Honorius III. The power of the order grew exponentially with these two appointments, and soon it became difficult for any single ruler to stand against the Knights of the Teutonic Order. Their political control over northern Europe was significant.

The Baltic

After the crusaders were defeated at Acre in 1291, the Teutonic Order moved its headquarters to Venice, and then to Marienburg, a major city in Prussia. This return home to German lands was a relief to the Teutonic Order and was greatly celebrated by the nation they called home. Internally, the order restructured its own government, turning to a theocracy instead of a feudal system and allowing themselves to be ruled by Priors and Abbots rather than Knight Generals.

In 1237, a newly-founded minor order in Livonia known as the Brothers of the Sword (*Schwertbroders*) joined the Teutonic Order as a supplicant. Livonia was subject to numerous revolts, uprisings, raids, and other violent activities, and, for that reasons, the Brothers of the Sword were seasoned and brutal fighters that were not afraid to lay down the dictates of the law in blood.

The Teutonic Knights fought primarily in northern Europe, and did not have much hold or authority on the Holy Land. They chose to defend Christians from heresy rather than hunting Muslims in the Holy Land; a different goal than their more expansionist brethren in other military orders. With help from Frederick II, the Baltic Crusades began, destroying many of the pagan tribes in the region and carving out a Baltic State for the Teutonic Knights to rule.

Initially, the Knights did very well in establishing their nation. Their military power and prowess destroyed the ill-prepared and poorly trained pagan tribes. Using superior fortifications and technology, they conquered all of Prussia and carved out sections of Livonia with ease, creating not only a Baltic State but also increasing the coffers of their own order as well as those of the Holy Roman Empire. But these crusades were not without a severe price: the pagan tribes did not surrender easily, and, even after an area was controlled, revolts and riots would break out and destroy the stability of the state. Knights were forced to burn and destroy the land, laying waste to the pagan tribes in order to ensure that stability would come to the new nation, and those bloody swaths were purchased with knightly lives. If a Knight was captured, he could expect horrible treatment; the natives hated the Knights so bitterly that they would skin them alive and/or offer them as sacrifices to their gods.

The nations of Poland and Lithuania, constant enemies of the order, became stronger in the late 14th and early 15th Centuries. In 1410, at Tannenberg, the Teutonic Order was crushed in battle by the military might of these two countries. Afterwards, the Teutonic Order lost a great deal of prestige and authority as well as a significant reduction in its military capabilities.

Organization

The Teutonic Order followed the lead of the Templars and Hospitallers by creating a system of provinces. They maintained a hierarchical chain of command with commanderies at the lowest level and Grand Masters at the apex. The Teutonic Knights ruled and organized themselves through a representative form of government, a unique development in the intrinsically feudalistic Middle Ages. The Grand Master of the Teutonic Knights was advised by these representatives of the commanderies and was required to gain the advice and consent of the chapter (the ruling body) when preparing to undertake a major action. The knights even ran elections, held once a year in the main house and in all provincial houses, in order to determine their governing body. Although the Grand Master was not an elected position in this manner, he could not act without the consent of the ruling body.

The officials of the Teutonic Order were known as (from lowest in the hierarchy to the most prominent) the commander (*Komtur,* preceptor), province commander (*Landkomtur*), national commander (*Landmeister*), and Grand Master (*Hochmeister,* magister). The highest leadership positions included the Grand Master, grand commander (*Grosskomtur*), marshal (*Ordensmarschall*), draper or quartermaster (*Trapier*), hospitaller (*Spittler*), and treasurer (*Tressler*), and were elected by the general chapter.

The knights lived communally, sleeping in dormitories on simple beds, eating together in a refectory, the fare modest and no more than was sufficient. Their clothes and armor were likewise simple but practical and their daily duties included training for battle, maintaining their equipment and working with their horses. The dignity of Master – the style of Grand Master came later – was elective for life, as in the Order of Saint John, and like all the great officers was limited to the professed knights. The Master's deputy, the (Grand)

Shield of the Teutonic Knights

Type: Large Metal Shield
AC Bonus: +2
Armor Check Penalty: 0
Arcane Spell Failure: 5%
Weight: 5 lbs

This shield bears no badge and is a simple, jet-black steel shield with no other markings or distinction. The individual bearing it may choose to set the shield against a charge, negating the impact and bonuses ordinarily given to the charging individual. This may also shatter the charging individual's weapon (see the rules for damage to objects in the standard game). The shield is never harmed in this use.

Commander, to whom the priests were subject, governed the Order in the absence of his superior. The (Grand) Marshal, likewise immediately subordinate to the Master, was in command of the knights and ordinary troops and was responsible for insuring they were properly equipped. The (Grand) Hospitaller was in charge of the sick and the poor, the Drapier was responsible for buildings and clothing, and the Treasurer administered the property. Each of these latter offices was generally held for shorter terms, rotating annually. As the Order expanded across Europe, it became necessary to appoint Provincial Masters for Germany, then Prussia, and later Livonia with a hierarchic structure paralleling the great offices.

Arms of the Brothers of the Sword

Livonian Brothers of the Sword were Livonian Knights allied with the German military and religious order but founded independently in 1202 by Bishop Albert of Livonia. As an independent brotherhood, they wore a different coat of arms, and held different standards. Their habit was a white robe with a red cross and sword.

The Brothers of the Sword were, if anything, more bloodthirsty than their companions in the Teutonic Order. In 1558, Czar Ivan IV of Russia invaded their territories, which were eventually partitioned between Russia, Poland, and Sweden. In 1561, the knights were disbanded; their Grand Master became the First Duke of Courland under Polish suzerainty. However, the knights retained their vast estates in the Baltic, and their violent and cruel tyranny continued for many generations.

A Knight of the Order

Teutonic Knights were always descended from German or northern European stock and usually had fair hair, pale skin, and light eyes. They were hardened military men, usually with thick musclesand broad physical structure, and their horses were short and burly to bear the weight of the knights and their armaments. They were fierce warriors, eager combatants, and always ready to eliminate the pagan threat from Christian lands. Rather than seeking out the Muslims or attempting to free the Holy Land, however, they centralized their assaults and energies toward ridding northern Europe of non-Christian tribes.

Arms

The Teutonic Knights wore a blue mantle charged with a black cross, which was occasionally worn over a white tabard or white mail. The arms of the order were a black cross on a blue and white field. Later, after the Teutonic Knights relocated to Prussia, the emblem of the order became a cross potent sable, placed within the escutcheon of the Holy Roman Empire.

The flag of the Teutonic Knights was a black cross on white field, usually shown with half of the flag cut into three ribbons (up to the center). Also, the flag is sometimes shown with a narrow blue stripe along the hoist.

How Do I Join?

Knights who sought to join the Teutonic Order had to be of German birth (although this rule was occasionally relaxed), a unique requirement among the Crusader Orders. Their nobility had to be without question (usually two to three ancestors in the paternal line), and they had to be capable of paying for their own livery and steed. The membership of this mostly German-speaking order was composed of various, distinct classes: knights, priests, and other brothers (lay brothers, with professional skills that assisted the order in numerous ways). A large number of people supported the order, ranging from auxiliary knights (the Brothers of the Sword, for example) to slaves. The order provided attendants called squires *(knechte)*, and sergeants-at-arms to maintain the commanderies and lesser soldiers in the army of the Teutonic Knights. These foot soldiers were usually coerced from the local peasantry, sometimes through violent threat or bloody "persuasion." The order owned many serfs and slaves.

Benefits of Membership

All members of the Teutonic Knights gain a +4 Class Bonus to Heal checks as a result of their affiliation with caring for the sick and the poor. However, they also gain the ability to cast True Strike once per day – a measure of their martial prowess.

Chapter 9: Knights of the Garter

The Order of the Garter was established by King Edward of England in the early 14th Century, bringing 25 of the most outstanding military leaders of the country to the side of their sovereign. This order began as a means of marking and securing alliances; it also established a new fellowship in religious worship "to the honor of Almighty God, the glorious Virgin Saint Mary and Saint George the Martyr." Those individuals that joined the order were not expected to be soldiers but tacticians and close allies of the throne of England.

It is thought that King Edward III was initially inspired by the legend of King Arthur and the Knights of the Round Table and therefore wished the Order of the Garter to consist of 24 knights – the number at Arthur's table. However, he created the order with 25 Knights Companion, one of whom was the Prince of Wales (also known as the Black Prince). These founding knights were primarily military men, skilled in battle and tournaments. While some were courtiers (though mildly experienced in the French campaigns), all of them were intensely loyal to the king. Three were foreigners to English soil, who had previously sworn allegiance to the English king and whom Edward trusted implicitly.

History

According to the histories of the Order of the Garter, the occasion of its birth was during a grand ball given by the English king. During the ball, a woman known as the "Fair Maid of Kent," suspected to actually be Joan, Countess of Salisbury, dropped a garter upon the floor as it fell from beneath her dress. She was dancing with the King at the time, and such a severe embarrassment and breach of etiquette was shocking. But the King, entranced with her and gallant to the end, picked up the garter and bound it on his own arm, remarking loudly, *"Honi Soit qui Mal y Pense"* ("Evil comes to him who evil thinks"). Thereafter, the King rebuilt the Castle of Windsor, said to have been originally constructed by King Arthur and decided to create an order of brotherly knights. They were to be called the Knights of the Blue Garter, keep loyal to England, and hold a grand feast each year on St. George's Day. Every June, the Knights of the Garter gathered at Windsor Castle, where the new inductees take the oath and are invested with the insignia of the order.

King Edward and his court spent a great deal of time modeling their new order after the Arthurian myth, holding elaborate pageants, jousting tournaments, and feasts. These events were appreciated by the peasantry and raised Edward's popularity among his people. The knights even met around circular tables, encouraging any and all parallels between their order and the ancient myth. The informal creation of this knighthood was formalized by

The Garter

There is another possible origin of the Order's name, and some historians insist that the story of the Fair Maid of Kent was invented by the French in order to make fun of the English Knights. According to some records, Richard I gave garters to certain knights as tokens of honor during his crusade. Other historians hypothesize that the circular garter was worn as an emblem of "unity and society." It was certainly a very suitable stylized heraldic device and a prominent identifier on mounted knights.

Edward's decree and official ratification on St. George's Day in 1348. Unusually, although the first founding members were male, women were also eligible for inclusion in the order nearly since its founding.

The garter was more than a symbol of the maiden of Kent or of France. It also served as a sign of the knights binding themselves together in common brotherhood. They were seen as the most loyal allies of the king, and they were expected to give their lives in his defense, using all of their abilities in his purposes. The patron saint of the Order of the Garter is St. George, the patron saint of soldiers, and the spiritual home of the order has therefore always been St. George's Chapel in Windsor Castle.

Although the Order of the Garter served in a military capacity, they were not usually sent into battle as other Orders of Knights. They were tournament knights, military tacticians, and advisors used as generals and support for political matters far more often than they were expected to contribute to wars, though they were perfectly capable on the battlefield.

Every knight is required to display a banner of his arms in St. George's Chapel. Each of the 26 knights that holds a position within the order is assigned a stall for this purpose. At the knight's death, the banner, crest, and mantling are taken away to be hung within his or her tomb or over the coffin during the funerary service. However, a small brass plate enameled with his or her arms is then affixed to the stall and remains in perpetuity, even as the stall itself is passed on to the next member of the order.

Removal from the Order

Although a number of Garter Knights were stripped of their ranks for crimes of heresy or cowardice, one of the main reasons that a knight was removed from the order during his or her lifetime was for treason. Members of the Order of the Garter were expected to be beyond reproach in their loyalty to England and its sovereign, but occasionally one was found to be traitorous. No mercy was given to the knight in this circumstance. Typically, such traitors were hanged or beheaded.

Some of these removals occurred during political revolutions, where a knight's loyalty to the rightful sovereign was misplaced (i.e., he backed the wrong heir) and the knight found himself on the losing side of a coup. Two of the most famous of these disgraced knights were Richard Nevill, Earl of Warwick, who was killed at the battle of Barnet in 1471; and Edward Stafford, 3rd Duke of Suffolk, who incurred the wrath of Henry VIII and was executed at the Tower of London.

The Seizure of France

While Edward III claimed loudly that the Order of the Garter was a revival of the Round Table, it is more likely that its formation was a move to gain support for his claim to the French throne. The motto of the order is a denunciation of those who think ill of some specific project and not a mere pious invocation of ill will upon evil-thinkers in general. Further, those who agree with this theory note that the colors of the garter are significant – blue embroidered with gold – those of the French Royal Arms. All things considered, it seems highly likely that the order originally represented the assembly of chivalry to aid King Edward of England in becoming King Edward of France.

Organization

The order of the Garter is comprised of the sovereign, the Prince of Wales, and 25 Knight Companions. Included in the insignia is a blue ribbon of velvet edged with gold and having a gold buckle. The pendant represents St. George slaying a fierce dragon. The accompanying certificate bears the well-known motto. The members are known as the Knights Companion, and are entitled to be called "Sir" or "Dame" and to add the letters, "K.G.," for Knight of the Garter to their names. In the case of a Lady Companion, the letters, "L.G.," are used after the surname or title. The leader of the order is always the English sovereign, and the knights have equal voice beneath his or her rule.

A Knight of the Order

Knights of the Order of the Garter rarely wear armor, but they occasionally choose to wear the cloak or habit of their order. Their garments are always very fine, as befits the noblest order of knights in England, and they are always members of noble stock and background. These knights appear far more as councilors than soldiers and are usually accompanied by an honor guard of servants and warriors to defend them on longer journeys.

The Sword of Grace

The Sword of Grace is a +1 Holy rapier, and conforms to the following stats:

Damage: 1d6 (plus Holy Damage of 1d6)

Crit: 18-20 x3

Range: —

Weight: 2 lbs

Type: Slashing

The Sword of Grace bestows one Negative Level on any Evil creature that attempts to wield it, which remains as long as the creature holds the weapon and disappears when it is discarded.

The wielder of the Sword of Grace can never be caught Flat-Footed so long as the weapon is by his or her side. Nor can his or her nobility be questioned – the person's aura seems to shine with purity and regal bearing that cannot be denied. The user may add an additional +2 bonus to Dexterity while the sword is unsheathed and can never lose his or her balance in any normal situation.

The sword further confers upon its user a certain panache and savoir-faire, which adds the character's Charisma Modifier to the following abilities: Balance, Forgery, Innuendo, and Search.

The Sword of Grace can never be used against the rightful Ruling Family of England or against faithful members of the Knights of the Garter, (whatever their Alignment may be) or against women of any kind who have not struck first. In these instances, the sword simply does no damage.

Armor of the Knights of the Garter

Type: Leather Armor

AC Bonus: +5 (+1 base, +4 enchantment)

Max Dex Bonus: +8

Armor Check Penalty: 0

Arcane Spell Failure: 5%

Speed: 30 feet

Weight: 15 lbs

A prestigious member (usually the second, as the head of the order is the King of England) of the Knights of the Garter is given this suit of light leather armor, suitable to wear as a doublet or covering beneath his or her cloak. It is designed to stop minor musket fire and to shatter thin rapiers before they can injure the bearer. The armor's origins are hidden in myth and legend, but the King of England once publicly claimed that it was created by Merlin of Camelot and that the old wizard's magic still protects the wearer of the suit.

The armor is a gorgeous brocade over leather shielding and is suitable for all formal and court occasions. Regardless of wear, the armor never fades, and the stitching appears as breathtaking and precise as the first day it was created. No harm can spoil the armor's manufacture; within 24 hours of receiving a cut or tear, it is renewed and the cut vanishes as if it never existed. The doublet is colored a magnificent jewel-toned blue, with symbols of golden dragons and circles (representing Arthur and the Round Table) embroidered upon the breast and the sleeves.

Arms

The emblem of the Order is a blue garter, worn either below the knee or at the bend of the right arm. Knights wear a formal collar made of gold, consisting of 26 red, enameled Tudor roses interspersed with 26 gold knots. In the center, is a pendant representing St. George and the Dragon. The roses and knots are placed alternately and joined to each other by gold links.

The insignia of the Order has gradually developed over the centuries, starting with a garter and badge depicting St George and the Dragon. A collar was added in the 16th Century with the star and broad ribbon being added in the 1800's. Although the collar could not be decorated with precious stones (the statutes forbid it), the other insignia could be decorated according to taste and affordability.

How Do I Join?

Members of the order only join at the invitation of the Sovereign of England. In order to be considered, one must be of "quality birth" and must have proven his or her loyalty in service to England. Knights are inducted only once a year, at the Feast of St. George in Windsor Castle.

Ladies of the Order

During the Middle Ages ladies were openly and fully associated with the order, although they did not enjoy all of the benefits of membership. One of the last medieval ladies to be honored was the mother of Henry VII and grandmother of Henry VIII, Lady Margaret Beaufort. After her death in 1509, the Order remained exclusively male for several generations, except for reigning queens as sovereign. This situation remained until 1901, when Queen Alexandra was made a Lady of the Order by Edward VII.

Benefits of Membership

The Knights of the Garter gain a +1 Class Bonus to all attacks against "a foe of England." Anyone who is an enemy of the English Crown falls into this classification.

The honor and prestige of the order, along with its association with the legend

of Arthur also empowers its members. Inductees receive a permanent +2 Class Bonus to their Charisma scores, and they may apply their Charisma Bonus to any Skill check they desire up to three times a day.

Chapter 10: Order of St. Michael

The enormous prestige that the Dukes of Burgundy had attained with their Order of the Golden Fleece rankled the King of France and inspired him to create his own order of knights as a rival. Charles, King of Burgundy, was a major threat to France, and the French king needed a buffer between his country and his enemy. The Order of St. Michael, also known as the Order of the Michaelmas, was to serve that purpose. In the beginning, it included 36 knights, who were to be elected into the order by the current members of the knighthood. In 1565, the number of knights was increased to 50 to give the order a greater amount of resources and to increase the number of the King's allies in all parts of France.

The abbey of Mont-Saint-Michel initially served as its seat of power. In 1555, it was transferred to the Ste Chapelle de Vincennes. In 1578, it finally moved to Paris. The order became an advisory council with full access to the king, eagerly offering its best advice on behalf of the noble courtiers and ranking royals of the country. Sadly, many of the French kings ignored the Order of St. Michael entirely, rarely calling upon its expertise or intelligence except when in dire need.

The French Order of St. Michael was established by Louis XI in 1469 as a response to the founding of the Burgundian Order of the Golden Fleece. Its creation coincided with the elimination of the remaining threat to the French Crown from the vassal princes or from England (at least until the Wars of Religion a century later). This step formalized the French Monarchy and established a standing army of knights – or *chevaliers* – whose purpose was to uphold the laws of France and protect the throne. It was also a step in the gradual erosion of the power of the nobility since these knights were completely dependant directly upon the Crown as opposed to the feudal structure that was rapidly dissolving in France. The foundation of the Order of Saint Michael by Louis XI represented the beginning of a new era between sovereign and subject.

Armor of the Knights of the Garter (cont'd)

The bearer of this armor always knows if someone in his presence is lying; further, they automatically know a true statement that might be spoken, no matter what that would be. The bearer of this armor is usually the King of England's choice for an advisor or diplomat in delicate situations, based on this unusual ability.

The Sword of Inspiration

The Sword of Inspiration is a +1 Holy longsword, and conforms to the following stats:

Damage: 1d8 (plus Holy Damage of 3d6)

Crit: 19-20 x2

Range: —

Weight: 3 lbs

Type: Slashing

The Sword of Inspiration bestows one Negative Level on any Evil creature that attempts to wield it. The Negative Level remains as long as the creature holds the weapon, and disappears when it is cast aside.

The Sword of Inspiration is not meant to be purely a combat item, although it is useful in a fight. Primarily, it is a weapon of prowess and esteem rather than a martial sword, and those who are granted the right to wield one are known to be very high in the King of France's esteem. Like a badge of office or a mark of honor, these swords are given only to those of the purest lineage and most faithful actions.

The Sword of Inspiration is a friend to artists and politicians of all sorts. While it is at its wielder's side, any speeches or artistic endeavors he or she attempts have a +2 Magical Bonus, and the lingering emotional effects last on its audience for an entire day. With this power, an artist can create a portrait that truly captures the regal feeling of the model, or a politician can convince an audience of his or her point of view and have it act.

Later, after the reign of Louis XIV, the Michaelmas was altered. Rather than being an advisory order, its purpose changed into an acclaim given to writers, to artists, or to magistrates who served France with exemplary courage and dedication. Its holders were known as *"chevaliers de l'Ordre du Roi."*

History

The Order was first proclaimed at a tournament in honor of the king's younger brother, the Duke of Berry. The statutes provided that the knights should meet annually, on the feast of its patron, the Archangel Michael (29 September), at the chapel of the monastery of Saint Michael off the Normandy coast.

King Louis went through the motions of asking the other knights of the order before making appointments but did not seriously take their word on the matter. The Order of St. Michael was essentially a "trophy order" created by the king as a showplace for his allies and those he favored. However, unlike many other orders, the sovereign undertook several responsibilities towards the companions, particularly giving them "competent and reasonable pensions" and acknowledging them before all others in honors, offices, and charges. These knights were songbirds in golden cages, expected to make the king look good and, in so doing, encourage the ideal of a stable and obedient France.

The first knights of St. Michael were representatives of some of the most ancient and powerful noble houses, although their selection was more probably due to the position of 12 of them as captains of the royal guard. Apart from the king's brother and his cousins, other knights appointed by Louis XI included members of most of the prominent families in France. Two nominees refused – one out of hostility, and the other because he had already been inducted into the Burgundian Order of the Golden Fleece and would theoretically have been in breach of those statutes if he joined the French order.

The increasingly wide distribution of the order, the number of persons admitted of relatively low estate and the failure of the sovereign to hold regular assemblies undoubtedly made it a less prestigious honor when compared to the Golden Fleece and the Garter. Although the formal limit on members was increased to 50 in 1565, this number was routinely exceeded by the French kings as they sought to give greater and greater gifts to their fading allies.

By the time Henri III ascended in 1574, there were as many as 700 living knights of Saint Michael, ranging from foreign monarchs down to bourgeoisie of modest origins. Henri III recognized the urgent need to reform the Order, renewing its vows and making it more prestigious and elite. This was a dangerous proposition and meant that the king needed to distance several hundred allies by not including them in the new order's formation, but Henri desperately needed to do so if the new order was to be given any respect in Europe.

When he founded the Order of the Holy Spirit in 1578, Henri III established a two-tier system of reward: the new order would be given to foreign and to French princes, to great nobles and very distinguished servants of the Crown, while the older Order of Saint Michael would be used to recognize service to the crown by lesser nobles and bourgeoisie. The number of members of the Order of the Holy Spirit was extended to a limit of 100, and that number remained constant thereafter.

A Knight of the Order

The knights of the Order of St. Michael were bound by an irrevocable oath of fidelity to France. This vow was given to every knight that was inducted, and, if broken, resulted in beheading. The order's members were often called the "Ever-loyal," although they were rarely so in actuality. Courtiers at heart, the knights of St. Michael dressed lavishly and kept up appearances in court but were routinely beheaded for treason when the Royal Whim decreed it.

Arms

The badge of the order was an image of St. Michael standing on a rock (to represent Mont-Saint Michel) while in combat with the serpent. It is suspended from a gold collar made of cockles (the traditional badge of pilgrims traveling to holy places) tied to one another with a double knot. The statutes of the order provided that, in certain circumstances, the badge may be hung from a simple chain or suspended from a black riband. The order's motto was *Immensi tremor Oceani.*

How Do I Join?

The Kings of France inducted members into the Order of St. Michael at their desire, cursorily checking with existing members as they saw fit and occasionally not even bothering to deal with such pleasantries. The Order of Saint Michael later became an award for artists, artists, doctors, and others who had distinguished themselves in the royal service outside the military sphere. Louis XIV permitted the maximum number of members to exceed 100 on occasion but his great-grand son and successor, Louis XV, kept carefully to the limit, while admitting a far higher proportion of non-nobles or newly ennobled gentlemen than any previous sovereign.

The Sword of Inspiration (cont'd)

The Sword of Inspiration can never be used against Lawful Good creatures nor against faithful members of the Knights of St. Michael (whatever their Alignment may be). In these instances, the sword will simply bend and break rather than causing harm.

Caster level: 9th

Prerequisites: Craft Magic Arms and Armor, Bless, creator must be of Good Alignment

Market Price: 36,000 gold

Armor of the Knights of St. Michael

Type: Full Plate Armor

AC Bonus: +9 (+8 base, +1 enchantment)

Max Dex Bonus: 0

Armor Check Penalty: -3

Arcane Spell Failure: 25%

Speed: 20 feet

Weight: 30 lbs

This suit of armor was created for the Order of St. Michael by the King of France and is a highly ornate and elaborate suit. Created more to be flashy and draw attention than to be truly serviceable or comfortable, the suit is rarely worn in court – and almost never worn in battle.

The armor is a bright pale blue in color, enameled lavishly with gold filigree and large gold-plated images that rise from the chest plate like sculptures. The metal of the armor is very light steel, strong but burdened with all the artistic accoutrements that cover the surface of the plate mail. A long, sumptuous cloak of blue and gold flows from behind the armor and is actually attached to the shoulder plates – making fighting while in this suit nearly impossible. Those wearing the armor are always flanked from the rear, no matter what other factors are in play.

While wearing this armor, the individual has a +3 Charisma Bonus and is considered to be an entrancing and charming person. He also may Take 10 on any court-related Skill, whether he possesses it or not.

Benefits of Membership

Inductees into the Order of St. Michael gain a permanent +2 Bonus to their Charisma scores, owing to the great prestige associated with being a member. Essentially, membership in the order is a boon to one's social status.

Additionally, knights of the order may cast Charm Person once per day. This is less a casting of a spell and more an extraordinary amount of charm and grace conferred by being a member of the order.

Chapter 11: Knights of the Holy Sepulchre

The Knights of the Holy Sepulchre are also known as the Equestrian Order of the Holy Sepulchre of Jerusalem. The order is somewhat of a mystery to historians. Its origins have been disputed for centuries. Myths exist that the order was created by Christ or by his Apostles; others suggest that it was created by any number of saints and was directly blessed by God. Whatever the truth, the Knights of the Holy Sepulchre are surrounded by mystery, apocrypha, and unusual miracles since their inception.

The Knights of the Holy Sepulchre were one of the most revered independent orders of the Middle Ages, respected for their mysticism and their

Gnostic beliefs. However, many of the other orders of knighthood considered them heretics and agents of the devil, while the peasants of the Holy Land saw them as a godsend of mercy and justice.

History

The origins of the Knights of the Holy Sepulchre are most often told in this fashion: the guardians of Christ's Tomb saw a vision and heard God's voice commanding them to watch over the Holy Land. It may indeed be possible that these Knights originated as a kind of "honor guard" for the Holy Sepulchre of Christ and that they banded together into a brotherhood that eventually became the Knights of the Sepulchre. While this theory seems plausible, there is no contemporary evidence of any kind to support such a claim. Certainly a religious Order of Canons of the Holy Sepulchre was founded early in the 12th Century, and this order soon established itself across Europe and acquired great wealth. There are no contemporary documentary sources, however, that demonstrate that these Canons assumed a military function or that a group of military brothers dedicated specifically to the protection of the Holy Sepulchre was associated with them.

The Order of Canons was an important institution and was often compared to the Hospitallers and Templars. Although the other orders were military monks and not peace-givers, the three orders were extremely powerful and respected in the Holy Land. Still, it cannot be said for certain that the Canons and the Holy Order of the Sepulchre were the same order at that time, or that the Holy Order of the Sepulchre were fulfilling a military function. It is more likely that they were peaceful monks and doctors ministering to the physical and spiritual needs of the Holy Land. Certainly, the Knights of the Holy Sepulchre were proselytizers, converting thousands of Muslims and pagans to their Christian cause.

The Canons of the Holy Sepulchre established priories, convents, and churches in Catalonia, Aragon, Perugia, Sicily, Germany, Poland, England, and Flanders. Following the fall of Jerusalem, the order became fragmented; the Superior of the convent took the title of "General of the Order," later claiming the style of "Grand Prior." By the mid-15th Century, the use of the title of "Master" of the Holy Sepulchre by the Superior at Perugia was generally recognized in most of Christian Europe, and the Knights of the Order of the Holy Sepulchre were beginning to turn from a purely ministering order into a more militant knighthood.

The Order of the Holy Sepulchre inducted its knights at first only within the Holy Land. They were primarily Crusaders, many of whom joined the order to minister, not to fight, and were for the most part handicapped by age or battle wounds. Still, the order was not designed to be of great military significance, using its skills to tend the sick and to study the Gnostic mysteries of the Holy Land and Christianity. Many of the knights were accepted into the order only to immediately retire to a life of prayer and contemplation at the Tomb of Our Lord.

Each would-be Knight of the Holy Sepulchre

Shield of St. Michael

Type: Large Metal Shield

AC Bonus: +2

Armor Check Penalty: 0

Arcane Spell Failure: 5%

Weight: 5 lbs

This shield is little more than a fancy strip of metal, carved and enameled with the sigils of France and the blazon of the Order of St. Michael. Beyond that, it has little powers of abilities other than its innate beauty and lightness. It typically accompanies the Armor of the Knights of St. Michael so as to enhance the beauty of the wearer.

The Sword of Faith

The Sword of Faith is a +3 Holy greatsword, and conforms to the following stats:

Damage: 2d6 (plus Holy Damage of 1d6)

Crit: 19-20 x2

Range: —

Weight: 1 lb

Type: Slashing

The Sword of Faith bestows two Negative Levels on any evil creature that attempts to wield it, which remain as long as the creature holds the weapon and disappears when it is cast aside.

The wielder of the Sword of Faith gains additional access to the following spells per day:

1st Level: Protection from Evil x2, Cure Light Wounds

2nd Level: Aid, Cure Moderate Wounds x2

3rd Level: Magic Circle against Evil, Cure Serious Wounds x2

4th Level: Divine Power, Cure Critical Wounds

The sword must constantly be at his or her side for it to grant this benefit. If it leaves the character's side for any reason, he or she no longer has access to any spells for the remainder of the day.

The Sword of Faith can never be used against Good creatures or against faithful members of the Knights of the Holy Sepulchre (whatever their Alignment may be). In these instances, the sword simply does no damage at all against the opponent.

had to affirm the nobility of his four grandparents and maintain sufficient means to maintain himself in the appropriate style. Further, and unusually, he must also be able to read and write as well as assist with studies and research into holy documents and backgrounds. The Knights of the Holy Sepulchre were very serious about their work, both in proselytizing and in documenting and researching the Gnostic cause.

Pope Clement VI appointed the Franciscans as the Guardians of the Holy Sepulchre in 1312, although it wasn't until 20 years later that they were able to establish a religious house at the Tomb. The first record of a military knight is dated 1336 and concerns Wilhelm von Boldensel, who traveled to Jerusalem and there received the honor of knighthood at the Tomb. The 14th and 15th Centuries represent the last great flowering of European chivalry and for many nobles, both great and modest, their knighthood was incomplete without receipt of the accolade at the Tomb. It became a pilgrimage site for many European nobles, and, more importantly, the Tomb and its guardians were respected and admired by the other knighthoods.

Many knights traveled to the Tomb of the Holy Sepulchre because they felt that doing so "crowned their knightly rank"; others journeyed there because they felt that it was a sign of a "good and true knighthood" rather than merely acquiring knighthood by caste or rank. There was a vast difference in their minds between knighthoods bestowed simply because of noble title, and in those men chosen by God to serve Him as true and honest knights. To travel to the Tomb was a sign that one intended to dedicate his life and soul not simply to God, but also to one's knighthood in God's service.

To be on their knees before the Tomb of Christ and to be invested there with knighthood by one of the Knights of the Holy Sepulchre in honor of Jesus and under the patronage of Saint George was the most holy and sacred privilege, conferring a very special dignity. The exact description of what this honor meant was less precise than that conceded to knights of the great military religious orders. The Knights invested at the tomb were sometimes called "Knights of Celestial Jerusalem," and they were much revered across Europe, no matter to which order of knighthood they belonged. A pilgrim to the Holy Land underwent an extremely testing ordeal simply to complete the journey. It is certain that such an expedition would not have been undertaken lightly, and those who managed to make it there and back safely were few in number.

As insignia of their rank, Knights of Celestial Jerusalem wore a chain with a medallion bearing the Jerusalem Cross. The earliest portrait of a knight, Willem de Jauche (1374), is a 16th Century drawing after a lost original and shows him wearing a chain made entirely of medallions bearing the Jerusalem Cross. Some Knights of Celestial Jerusalem also wore the cross embroidered on their clothes, but it is not certain that the privilege of wearing this cross was a sign of knighthood or a badge of the pilgrimage.

That the history and development of what came to be defined as an Order of Chivalry is so uncertain in the early years is hardly surprising. Unlike the Templars, Hospitallers and Teutonic Knights, the Holy See did not agree that the Holy Sepulchre knights were members of a Religious Order of the Church. There was a great deal of argument as to whether the order was a religious group, a monastic order, or a militant one, and the charges of Gnosticism plagued the Knights of the Holy Sepulchre throughout their existence, removing much of the support they might otherwise have gained from their work.

Organization

The knights of the Holy Sepulchre were loosely organized and, other than their "Grand Prior," had no apparent leadership. Most of the Knights lived in monasteries or hospices, studying ancient texts or tending to the sick. Many of them were members of other orders, joining the Knights of the Holy Sepulchre when they were considered too old or infirm to continue on the battlefield. They were never particularly numerous but

Armor of the Knights of the Holy Sepulchre

Type: Full Plate Armor

AC Bonus: +9 (+8 base, +1 enchantment)

Max Dex Bonus: +3

Armor Check Penalty: -3

Arcane Spell Failure: 25%

Speed: 20 ft

Weight: 30 lbs

This magical suit of armor was forged by the first Grand Master of the Knights of the Holy Sepulchre. Supposedly, it was forged from a strain of iron found within Christ's Tomb, and the remnants of one of the three nails used to crucify Jesus was incorporated into its steel.

The armor is often worn by the Grand Master, although, on rare occasions, it is sometimes donned by a Champion or other prestigious member of the order. It remains within Jerusalem and never leaves the city's environs and outlying plains. The armor is considered one of the most sacred relics of the order.

The armor is sterling silver in color, inlaid with green and blue tracings across the shoulders and breastplate. The front plate of the armor is emblazoned with the blue cross of the Knights of the Holy Sepulchre and appears to be clean and pure no matter the difficulties surrounding it. The individual within the armor always appears to be relaxed and at peace under any circumstances. When wearing this armor, the individual may Take 10 on any non-combat roll, even if the character would not ordinarily have the time to do so.

kept themselves small and elite; those who entered had to be noble, genuine in their beliefs and intents, and able to read and write (a rare talent in the Middle Ages).

By the first half of the 15th Century, 130 knights existed in the order. Ninety-seven were German. Of the 503 Knights recorded during the second half of the century, 385 were German. While this may indicate that knighthood of the Holy Sepulchre was most sought after by German knights, the figures may have been distorted because more German documentary records have survived.

A Knight of the Order

While some writers of the Middle Ages considered the Knights of the Holy Sepulchre to be "superior of all other knights of the world," the majority of its knights were old men or weary monks performing dangerous duties in the plague-ridden Holy Lands. Still, for many knights who traveled thousands of miles on pilgrimage, their induction into the Order of the Holy Sepulchre or into the Knights of Celestial Jerusalem was a crowning achievement. Many of the knights who earned their spurs after an arduous pilgrimage and were re-dubbed upon the stairs to the Holy Tomb of Christ sincerely believed the honor to be of greater worth than knighthoods conferred on their contemporaries by local sovereigns.

Temporal authorities and the other knightly orders did not give any such special recognition to knights invested at the Tomb, and there is no evidence to suggest that the Knights of the Holy Sepulchre were in any way considered superior to the other orders.

How Do I Join?

As with all other knightly orders, the nobility of the candidate was extremely important. Circumstances in the Holy Land, however, meant that a candidate's nobility was attested by witnesses rather than proven by documents since few knights traveled to war with their family lineage and birth certificate in their saddlebags.

It's therefore likely that not all of the knights invested at the Tomb of the Holy Sepulchre were in fact of noble birth, although all were attested as such. One pilgrim in the records of the Holy Sepulchre described how he affirmed his noble standing for several days, being interrogated by the Knights of the Tomb at great length while he sat vigil at the opening of the Tomb.

A typical investiture at the Tomb of the Holy Sepulchre occurred in the following fashion. The evening before the ceremony, the candidate would make his confession. The dubbing ritual normally followed celebration of the Mass of St. George (the patron saint of knighthood) immediately after sunrise. The knight carrying out the investiture – usually the highest-ranking person present – would place the gold belt and sword around the new knight's waist, whereupon the latter would swear an oath to take up the sword in honor and devotion to God. Some chose to swear their oath to the Virgin or to St. George, offering their oath not to God Himself but through

Shield of the Knights of the Holy Sepulchre

Type: Large Metal Shield

AC Bonus: +3 (+2 base, +1 enchantment)

Armor Check Penalty: 0

Arcane Spell Failure: 5%

Weight: 5 lbs

This shield is painted with the image of Christ on the cross, the upper half against a gold background depicting the sun, and the lower appearing as a sea of blood. By spending a Partial Action, the bearer of this shield may Refocus, gaining all the benefits of that action.

an intermediary as was common in Catholic custom.

The knight swore to guard and defend the Holy Church against the enemies of the Faith, and to aid with all his power the Crusades within the Holy Land. The knights dubbed at the Tomb of the Holy Sepulchre were charged and obliged to guard and defend God's people and render justice, to study the Lord's Grace in all things, and to help the sick and the needy. In addition, they were commanded not to engage in treason against their rightful lords and to defend and protect widows and orphans.

After taking the sword from its scabbard, the candidate would kiss its pommel in submission and then return it to the investing knight. That knight routinely gave one to three touches on the shoulder or nape of the neck of the candidate being knighted, following which, the new knight would replace the sword in its scabbard.

He then put first his right foot on the tomb for another knight to attach a spur and then followed the same procedure with the left foot. The gold sword and belt would be unbuckled to be reused for the next investiture and was retained at the Tomb. There is no evidence that these rituals were adhered to rigidly or that the promises required of the knights were always identical. The ceremony was probably maintained in a similar fashion as candidates learning of the ritual from returning knights would expect a similar one for their own investitures.

Benefits of Membership

Knights of the Holy Sepulchre have the ability to cast Bless and Bane three times per day. Note that the knight may cast a total of three spells per day. Thus, he may cast Bless three times, Bane three times, or any combination of the two. He cannot cast both spells three times a day.

Once per day, the members of this order may also cast Cure Light Wounds as though they were Clerics of half their Character Levels.

Chapter 12: Minor Orders

The previous chapters have covered some of the most important and influential knightly orders throughout history. However, there are a great number of minor orders that flourished as well. A few of these are detailed below.

Order of the Tower and the Sword

The Military Order of the Tower and the Sword (also known as the Order of Valor, Loyalty, and Merit) traces back its roots to an order of chivalry created by King Dom Afonso V, in 1459, on the occasion of his conquests in North Africa. The order is Portuguese in origin and is an honorary one reflecting bravery on the battlefield. The order is occasionally given to those men of low birth who distinguish themselves in the King's service and is considered one of the only means by which a low-born individual can gain access to court.

The Military Order of the Tower and the Sword grew rapidly, becoming the highest of Portuguese non-military orders. After the conquest of Granada in 1492, when there were no more Moors to fight, the order was awarded for exceptional service to the Crown in other arenas such as in the highest offices of government, courts of justice, or in the command of troops in campaign, for military or civic deeds of heroism, and to reward outstanding acts of abnegation and sacrifice for Portugal or humanity. It was highly regarded by the royalty of Portugal, and there were many members of the order that were formally accepted as advisors and councilors to the king.

Order of Avis

The Order of Avis was originally a militia of knights created by the King of Castile sometime after 1166. The initial intent of the order was to secure the defense of the recently re-captured city of Évora in Northern Africa. The knights of the Order of Avis did not live within the boundaries of Castile but instead patrolled outside its borders, protecting Castilian interests and holdings and also gathering information on their Moorish enemies.

Originally, the order formed a militia to defend Calatrava from the Moors, assisting the Knights of Calatrava. Eventually, they moved into Moorish territory, taking the fight deep into the territory of their enemies and fighting battles within Moorish kingdoms.

The order was a monastic-military one, and all of the knights were committed to vows of poverty, chastity, and obedience. They were further ordered to fight the Moors on their own battlefields and to extend the domain of Castile into Moor-occupied territories. In 1211, the King of Portugal, Dom Afonso II, donated the town of Avis to the order, and they became entirely separate from the Calatrava knights. The Master had the town fortified and a castle and a convent built. Henceforth, the militia became known as the Order of Avis.

The Order of Avis was a very peasant-class knighthood. For this reason, it was looked down upon by other orders of knighthood, even though they faced incredible danger on their forays into the Moorish lands. Politically, the order depended only upon the Kings of Portugal and had no Papal blessing upon its organization.

After the campaign that seized the Kingdom of Granada and effectively destroyed Moorish influence in and around Spain, the Order of Avis was able to rest upon its laurels. Soon after, the knighthood was turned into an honorary order by the King of Portugal, but it

Arms of the Order

The Order has five classes of membership, each representing a different rank of duty: Grand–Cross, Grand Officer, Commander, Officer, and Knight or Dame. Any member of the order may wear its arms, but only the top two ranks (Grand-Cross and Grand Officer) may wear the badge of the knighthood.

The Ribbon is light blue. The Badge of the Order is a five-pointed silver cross edged with gold, encircled by an oak wreath of green, edged and fruited gold. The cross bears at the center a sword encircled by a green and gold oak wreath. Over all is the motto, *"Valor Lealdade e Mérito"* in letters of gold.

The Star of the Order is a five-pointed chipped star of gold which is only worn by the Grand Officer- or Grand-Cross-ranked knights. The Commander class wears a similar star in silver, but at the center is the Badge of the Order without the oak wreath.

has always retained its fierce nature and devotion to battle. Only those who are being recognized for their service in the military or on the battlefield are allowed to join, and those nominated must be formally recognized as peers by the other members of the order before they can be inducted. The Military Order of Avis together with the Military Orders of Christ and of St. James of the Sword form the group of the "Ancient Military Orders," having a Chancellor and a Council of eight members appointed by the President of the Republic to assist him as Grand-Master in all matters concerning the administration of the Order.

Organization

The order can only be conferred on officers within the Portuguese Army or on military units, both Portuguese and foreign, for outstanding military service. Those Portuguese who are already members of another knightly order can still be inducted into the Order of Avis; such service is not seen as conflicting in any way.

The Order has five classes: Grand-Cross; Grand Officer; Commander; Officer; Knight or Dame, although women were not inducted into the order until much later in history. The Grand-Cross is the leader of the order, and the position is always filled by the current King of Portugal. Second in power to the Grand-Master was the Grand-Commander – a position always filled by the Crown Prince.

Arms

The Badge of The Order, which varies in size according to the rank and classification of the individual wearing it, is a green-enameled cross fleury edged in gold. The Avis Order occasionally uses a green cross that is hollow or bears the sigil of the Portuguese King. The Star of the Order, worn only by those of Grand Officer rank or higher, is an eight-pointed one in gold charged in the center with the Badge of the Order upon a field of silver within a garlanded laurel wreath in gold. The Commander class wears a similar star in silver, but the center of the star is the badge of the order with no wreath. Both stars are set upon a ribbon of plain green.

Order of the Holy Ghost

The Hospitallers of the Holy Ghost were an organization within the Holy Land that took on the appearance of an order of knighthood, were granted vows and orders from the pope, yet never lifted a sword. In fact, they were more pacifistic an order of knights than any other in the world, and they refused to strike down another person even in defense of their own lives.

Many different kings and popes attempted to give a military character to the Hospitallers of the Holy Ghost, but the knights of that order never earned arms nor had occasion to use them. The official creation of the Order of Hospitallers of the Holy Ghost was enacted by Pope Innocent III. The knights of the order were inspired by an example given by a knight of Castile, who established a lay community for the care of the sick under the patronage of the Holy Ghost. The patronage of the Holy Ghost was an unusual one, and it is not known why the knights invoked it.

They held a series of simple hospices, caring for the sick and needy in all parts of the world, not simply within the Holy Land. Their first hospital building was erected in the heart of Rome, beneath the watchful and curious eyes of the pope and his dignitaries.

In the beginning, the institution was in lay hands, with Innocent III confining himself to attaching to it four clerics for spiritual duties. These officials were responsible only to the pope or his delegate. In return, he endowed the knights with the most extensive privileges, hitherto reserved for the great monastic orders: exemption from all spiritual and temporal jurisdiction save his own and the rights to build churches, to nominate chaplains, and to have their own cemeteries.

Later, Pope Paul V altered the purposes and commands of the Order of the Holy Ghost, dividing the order into several different factions and attempting to break it apart and absorb the little knighthood into the Church entire. He further attempted to distribute brevets of the knighthood to men of all classes – to laymen, often married, which gave rise to protests on the part of the religious knights of the order. Such dissention nearly destroyed the Knights of the Holy Ghost, but, in the end, they were successful in maintaining both their autonomy from the Church and their unity.

Order of the Dragon

The Order of the Dragon (German *"Drachenorden"* and Latin *"Societatis draconistrarum"*) was an institution modeled on the Order of St. George. The order was first installed in 1408, and the first knight was dubbed by the Holy Roman Emperor Sigismund, mainly for the purpose of gaining protection for the imperial family. According to its statute, the order also required its initiates to defend the Cross and to do battle against its enemies, principally the Turks. The original order comprised 24 members of the nobility, including such notable figures as King Alfonso of Aragon and Naples, and Stefan Lazarevic of Serbia.

In 1431, Emperor Sigismund called together a number of powerful princes and vassals – allies and those he wished to make allies. These men were strong in their own right, and many of them owed no allegiance to the Holy Roman Empire. Still, Sigismund hoped to use them to increase his own power and ensure peace in the region. He intended to do this by giving them all a sign of unity and by encouraging them to think of one another as more than allied princes but also as brothers brought together within an order of knighthood. He thought this would make them more easily controlled and unified. Therefore, the Order of the Dragon was enlarged and expanded, and Emperor Sigismund "sold" its honors in exchange for unity within and surrounding his empire.

One of the most famous members of the Order of the Dragon was Vlad Dracul of Wallachia, father of the infamous Vlad Dracula, the Impaler (see Avalanche Press's VLAD THE IMPALER for the story of Vlad and his son). Vlad was a strong claimant for the throne of the principality of Wallachia, and, without his support, Emperor Sigismund might have lost significant territory to invading Turkish hordes. At the time, Vlad was serving in the city of Sighisoara as frontier commander, guarding the mountain passes from Transylvania into Wallachia. In exchange for his induction into the Order of the Dragon, Vlad received Sigismund's pledge to support his claim to the throne of Wallachia.

The Order of the Dragon adopted a winged dragon as its symbol in 1408. The image would soon become infamous throughout Wallachia and the Holy Roman Empire. Vlad was proud of this achievement, partly because being a knight gave a certain validity that his claim to the throne was lacking and partly because his new alliance with the Holy Roman Emperor would serve him exceptionally well. In fact, he was so pleased with himself that he had new Wallachian coins minted, all of which show on one side a winged dragon – the symbol of the order. Further, Vlad's personal coat-of-arms incorporated a dragon, and he had dragon icons brought in to decorate his castle and sewn upon his clothing.

The dragon was intended to convey a favorable image. When drawn from medieval iconography in which the dragon represents the Beast of Revelation (Satan) who is slain by the forces of good (Christianity), it shows that humanity's strength is stronger than Satan's power. Although the beast itself is evil, it is an evil which can be conquered and must be overcome. It is unclear if Vlad truly understood these subtle meanings, for he took on the nickname "Dracul," supposedly in reference to his induction into the order – though many of his peasants took it to mean that he was turning to the Great Beast, that is, to Satan. The name is alternately translated "devil" and "dragon."

His son Vlad used the sobriquet, "Dracula," or "Son of the Dragon." But again, it was often mistaken by the peasant class as meaning "Son of the Great Beast." And certainly, the peasants of Wallachia believed that their leader was taken by the Great Beast when the impalings and other horrors began. Still, Vlad (as his father did) used the term as a sign of honor and bore it proudly and bravely. On a number of occasions, Vlad signed documents using the name "Vlad Dracula," and he rapidly grew famous by that name. Slowly, as his reign grew bloodier, the word "Dracula" took on more and more superstition and fear. More information on Vlad is available in Avalanche Press's VLAD, THE IMPALER: BLOOD PRINCE OF WALLACHIA.

After the death of Sigismund in 1437, the Order of the Dragon lost much of its prominence, though its iconography was retained on the coats-of-arms of several noble families.

Arms

The symbol of the Order of the Dragon was the image of a circular red or black dragon with its tail coiled around its neck. On its back, from the base of its neck to its tail, was the red cross of St. George on the background of a silver field. With the expansion of the order, other symbols were adopted, all variations on the theme of dragon and cross. Other emblems included a necklace and a seal, each with a variant form of the dragon motif.

Order of the Swan

The Order of the Swan was a brotherhood of knights not directly related to any temporal government or nation. They were created and indulged by the pope in 1440 and organized to serve the purposes of the Catholic Church instead of working through the system of government. Originally, the Order of the Swan was comprised of 30 gentleman and seven ladies, united to "pay special honor to the Blessed Virgin."

The organization was not at all militant in nature, although many of its members were from the soldierly class of noble. It spread rapidly, numbering about 330 members in 1464 in addition to branches established in several other countries, including northern Europe (the traditional homeland of fiercely violent and tyrannical orders such as the Teutonic Order in Prussia).

Those who swore their fealty to the Order of the Swan had the pope's full indulgence for all sins they committed while in his service; some took this quite literally, and became assassins for the papacy. Others were ambassadors, negotiators, or spies.

Arms

All those who served the Order of the Swan wore the same emblem: a silver or white swan on a grey ribbon. The order's badge was rarely worn on clothing or emblazoned on shields, but several of the noblemen that served its cause had the swan worked into their personal arms and livery.

Order of the Bath

The Order of the Bath was a prestigious English knightly order founded during the Enlightenment. It was established by King George I in 1725 and conferred as a reward either for military service or for exemplary civilian merit. The order was very prestigious, and those inducted were considered to be very high among the nobles of the kingdom – higher in some cases than ranking noblemen of good lineage.

Before induction into the order, knights spent the evening being bathed in an elaborate

Little-known Orders

There are a host of obscure orders that existed through the Middle Ages and at other times. A few of these are listed below.

* *The Sword:* founded by Guy of Lusignan, King of Cyprus, in 1192, disappeared with the conquest of Cyprus by the Turks in 1571
* *Saint Blasius:* in Armenia (13th c.-15th c.)
* *Saint-John and Saint-Thomas:* in the Middle East (1254)
* *Saint Thomas of Acre:* founded as a military order by Peter des Roches, Bishop of Westminster, in 1228
* *Mountjoy:* later known as Holy Redeemer and Montfragüe, founded in 1175 and merged with Calatrava in 1221
* *Our Lady of the Rosary:* in 1209 by the Archbishop of Toledo, extinct soon afterward
* *Our Lady of Mercy:* in 1233 in Aragon, played a part in the conquests of Valencia and Majorca but became a purely religious order in the 14th Century
* *Sant-Jordi d'Alfama:* by the king of Aragon in 1201 (merged with Montesa in 1399)
* *Concord:* in the 1240's by Ferdinand III of Castile, disappeared after his death in 1252,
* *Saint James of the Sword:* an offshoot of the Spanish order in Portugal in 1275
* *The Sword-Brethren:* created in 1197 by a citizen of Bremen, soon militarized by the Bishop of Riga and merged in 1237 with the Teutonic Order.

purification ritual, which had an intensely religious aspect and was likened to the bathing and baptism of John the Baptist. From the coronation of Henry IV (1399) to that of Charles II (1661), it became customary to create a certain number of knights during royal occasions of great brilliance. A formal occasion without an induction into the order was a slight to the occasion's host, and rarely did the King of England offend his councilors in that manner. The numbers of recipients of this honor, therefore, grew quite high. However, until George I formally organized the order, there was no organization into which these knighted individuals were inducted.

These revered Knights of the Bath took precedence over both landless knights-errant and landed knights bachelors. They were respected among counts and barons and considered extreme examples of nobility, charity, and civility among the English noble class. Originally, membership comprised a small number of entrants: the British monarch, a Great Master to lead the order, and 36 standing knights. Membership regulations have undergone numerous changes over the centuries. Three classes of knights were instituted, and civilian classes for low-born English natives of great gentility and courtesy were added as well, raising the number of members ever higher.

Investiture into the two highest classes (Knight Grand-Cross and Knight Commander) is certain induction into the noble courts of the King. The officers of the order are the Dean of Westminster, the Bath King-at-Arms, the registrar, the Usher of the Scarlet Rod, and the secretary. The Knights Grand-Cross of this order are allotted stalls in the order's chapel within Westminster Abbey, where their banners, crests, and coats of arms are affixed.

Arms

The badge of the order depicts three crowns with the order's motto, *"Tria juncta in uno,"* ("Three joined in one") as well as the Welsh motto, *"Ich dien"* ("I serve") and the emblems of England, Scotland, and Ireland (rose, thistle, shamrock).

Order of the Golden Fleece (Toison d'Or)

The Order of the Golden Fleece, also known as the *Order du Toison d'Or*, was created as a prestigious honorary order of knighthood by Philip of Burgundy. The order's popularity skyrocketed, and it was rapidly hailed as a crowning achievement of the king's lifetime. The knights of the order were given accolades from many countries, and numerous sovereigns attempted to replicate the feat by creating honorary orders of their own.

The Order of the Golden Fleece was a brotherhood, not of crusading knights but of courtiers with no other aim than to contribute to the splendor of the sovereign and the pleasure and culture of the realm. Their most serious business was the sport of jousts and tournaments. Completely unlike the other orders of knighthood before them, the Order of the Golden Fleece was a strange divergence, and a clear child of the "Age of Courtly Love."

The foundation of the Order of the Golden Fleece marked a revival of interest in chivalric institutions which had generally fallen into disregard. Rather than create an organization whose purpose was to defend the Christian states or drive off militant Muslims or Moors, the Order of the Golden Fleece was more of a superficial band of knights, designed to make a good show but not really go fighting anyone.

In 1396, the Burgundian army, accompanied by the best that French chivalry had to offer, suffered almost total destruction at the hands of the Turks. This crushing blow to chivalric arrogance crippled the knightly orders throughout Europe. The military importance of mounted knights, heavily and expensively armored, was much less significant against highly trained bowmen and foot-soldiers. With the crushing victories of the Welsh bowmen over twice their number of mounted knights, the use of such heavy fighters became *déclassé.* Tournament fighting became the only purpose for heavy armor and for jousting, with archers, crossbowmen and highly-trained pikemen taking over the battlefield on foot. With these changes, the heavy knight orders of the past fell into disarray and lost their prestigious reputations, eventually falling out of use entirely with their possessions and estates seized by the nations that once lauded them.

Philip's own order was in many ways similar to the Garter, also having written statutes precisely describing the duties and obligations of membership. The essential difference was that the obligations of the companions of the Golden Fleece towards their sovereign and each other were more extensive while the financial requirements were less stringent.

Arms

The Order of the Golden Fleece excluded all "heretics" (non-Christians, and in particular those who followed unapproved offshoots of Christianity) from joining. Even with this stricture, the order received a great deal of criticism about the very pagan nature of its emblem and badge. The name and badge of the order, a pendant sheep's fleece made of gold, was intended to represent the treasure sought by Jason and the Argonauts – an heroic legend which paralleled the Arthurian origins of the Order of the Garter. While this seemed initially simply to be a celebration of a heroic image of classical times, many servants of the Catholic Church planted heavy criticism on Burgundian shoulders for their choice of a pagan hero. To appease the Church, the Burgundian King and his Chancellors added the fleeces of Jacob, Mesa, Job, and David into the mythology and knightly background, tying the order more strongly to the Catholic Church and Christian beliefs. The Six Fleeces corresponded, according to the Burgundians, to the virtues of magnanimity, justice, prudence, fidelity, patience, and clemency.

The badge of the order is a single fleece (or, in some cases, six full fleeces) hung from a red ribbon. Knights of the Order typically wear their badge only to affairs of state or formal occasions.

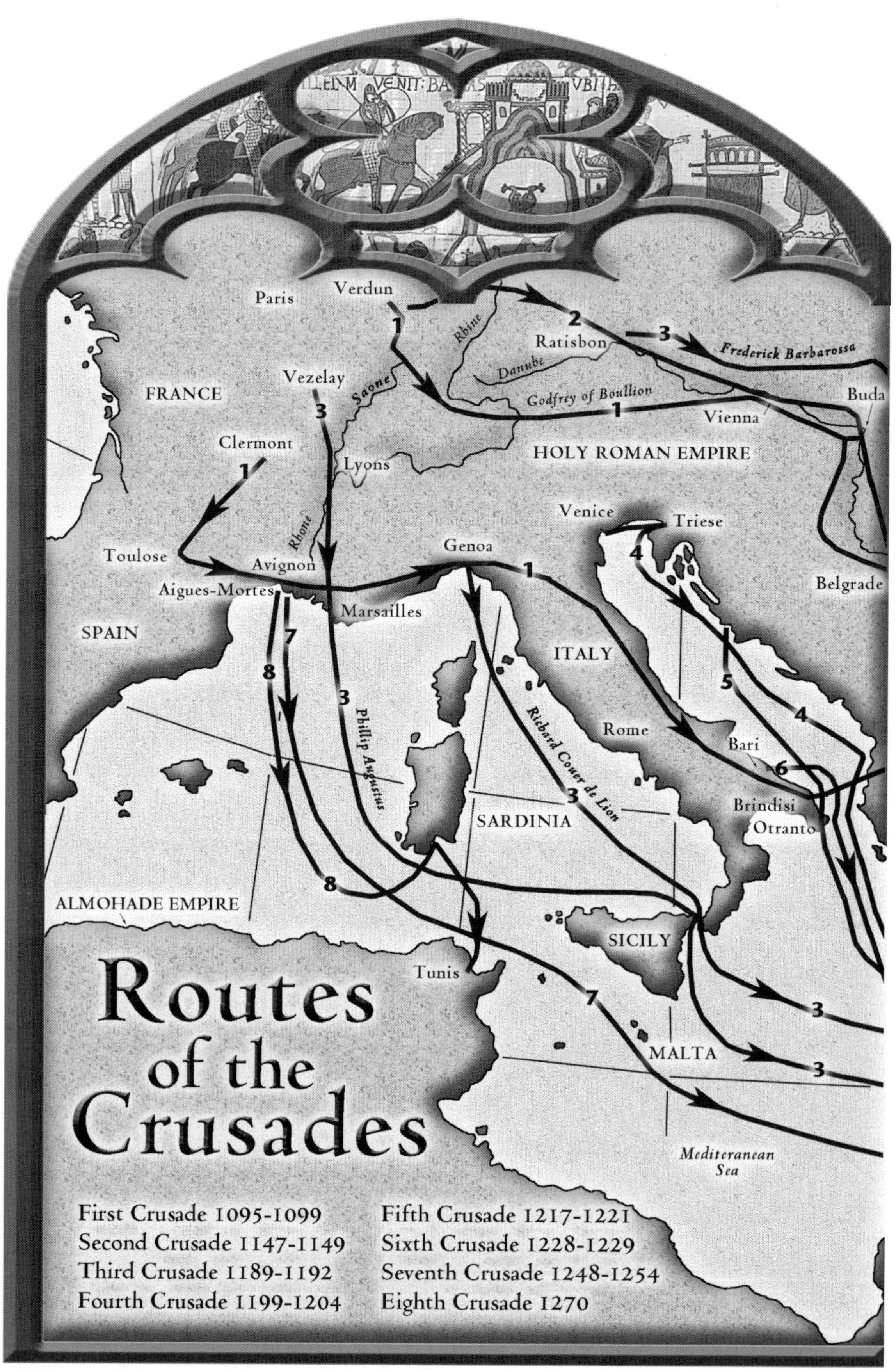
Paris
Verdun
Ratisbon
Frederick Barbarossa
Rhine
Danube
Vezelay
Saone
FRANCE
Godfrey of Boullion
Buda
Vienna
Clermont
Lyons
HOLY ROMAN EMPIRE
Venice
Triese
Rhone
Toulose
Avignon
Genoa
Aigues-Mortes
Belgrade
Marsailles
SPAIN
ITALY
Phillip Augustus
Richard Coner de Lion
Rome
Bari
Brindisi
Otranto
SARDINIA
ALMOHADE EMPIRE
SICILY
Tunis
MALTA
Mediteranean Sea
Routes of the Crusades
First Crusade 1095-1099
Second Crusade 1147-1149
Third Crusade 1189-1192
Fourth Crusade 1199-1204
Fifth Crusade 1217-1221
Sixth Crusade 1228-1229
Seventh Crusade 1248-1254
Eighth Crusade 1270

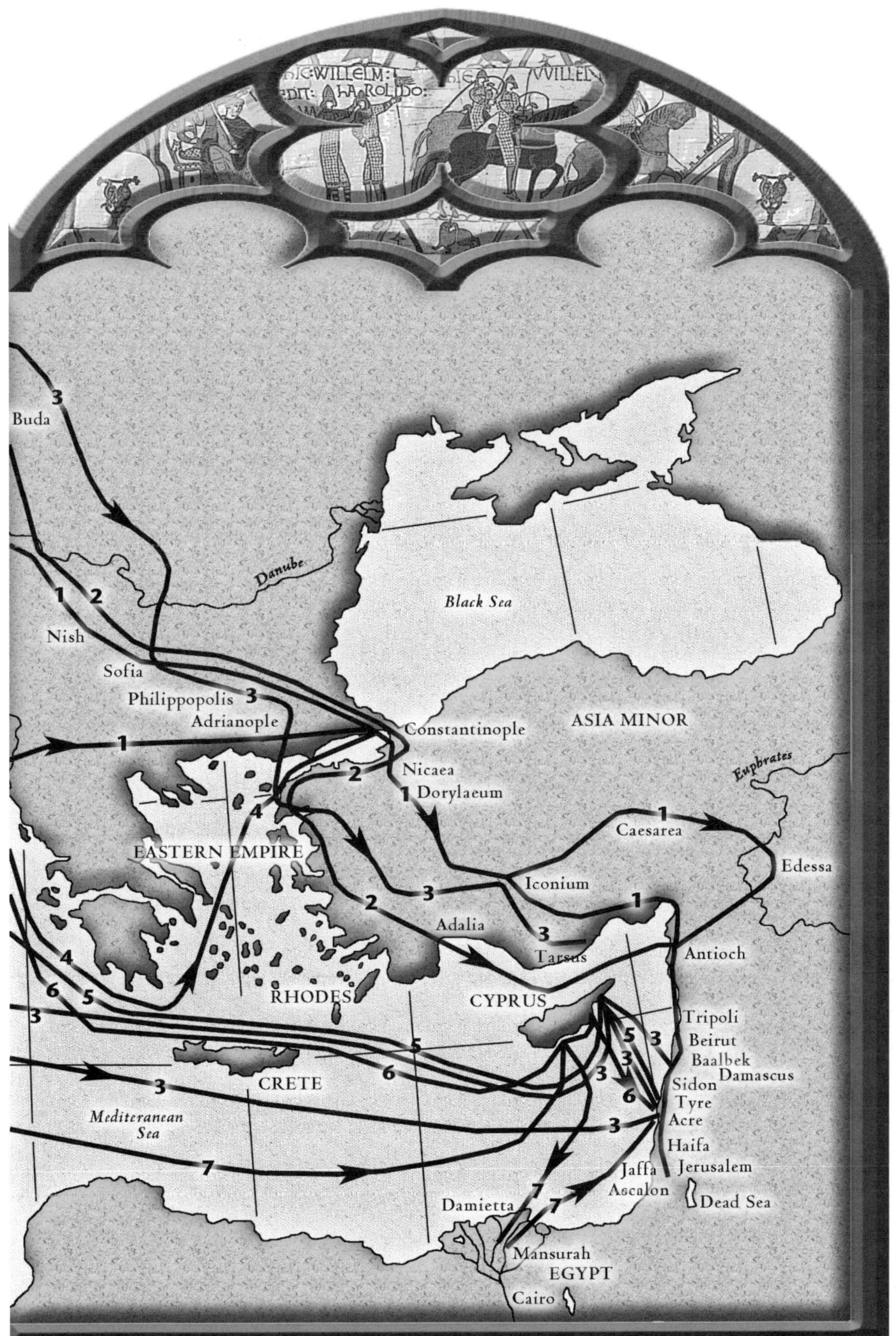

Buda
Danube
Black Sea
Nish
Sofia
Philippopolis
Adrianople
Constantinople
ASIA MINOR
Nicaea
Dorylaeum
Euphrates
Caesarea
Edessa
EASTERN EMPIRE
Iconium
Adalia
Tarsus
Antioch
RHODES
CYPRUS
Tripoli
Beirut
Baalbek
Damascus
Sidon
Tyre
Acre
Haifa
CRETE
Mediteranean Sea
Jaffa
Jerusalem
Ascalon
Dead Sea
Damietta
Mansurah
EGYPT
Cairo

Chapter 13: Creating Your Own Order

The Knightly Orders of history sprang up throughout the Holy Land as the Crusades of the Christian nations progressed. Without this galvanization, the noble society of the Middle Ages might never have spawned such a strange and unusual stratum. Knightly orders are both captured within the strict caste system of feudalism and simultaneously outside of it, protected by the Church and able to refuse orders of taxation from the nation's crown.

Knightly Orders rely on honor, dedication, and lineage in order to select their members. Most members of this style of organization are descended from certain "noble" lineages, and therefore are trained in the order's beliefs and morality from a young age. These members are carefully and secretly tutored to follow the methods and moral code of the knightly order even before they are allowed to know such an organization exists; therefore there are few traitors or dissatisfied members of their societies. Their hierarchical order is commonly based on time spent within the organization as well as military advancement dependent on skill and leadership potential.

These prestigious orders don't spring up without warning, nor are a group of knights – however noble – spontaneously considered a new order without formal recognition. To become an official knightly order, steps must be taken and the knights must be blessed and confirmed by both the noble head of state and by the pope. Only after achieving blessing and benediction from both these sources can a knightly order bear the arms and rights of separation.

Further, there is a monastic background to nearly all orders of knighthood. No matter how noble their first few members are, they must be willing to give up all land and title and join the humble brothers of the Church. From this vantage, they take up arms and fight for the interests of the Church (or join a medicinal order of hospitallers). Once they have proven themselves on this field, they gain the attention of the ruling class. After several more years of service (and, typically, the swearing of an oath as an order, dedicating themselves to some righteous goal), the knightly order is blessed and confirmed by papal bull and royal writ.

Any knightly orders you create for your campaign should follow a similar regimen. Even if you're running a fantasy campaign and therefore don't have a "pope," the order should remain tied to a key religious group. Otherwise, it is simply an elite guard or a pack of stormtroopers. Knights aspire, at least in name, to some loftier goal than simple service to the state.

Historical Period

Knightly Orders typically began in the period of expansion into the Holy Land, around the mid-11th Century. Because of the vast numbers of Christian pilgrims flocking to Jerusalem, warriors were needed to protect the roads and keep them clean of bandits and other dangers. These free-roaming soldiers banded together for greater effectiveness, and many of them dedicated their lives to this purpose. Defending pilgrims and protecting the faithful are common origins for such fraternities, and many knightly orders began their careers under just such humble scenarios.

Another common means of beginning a knightly order is to set the foundation of the group within a pre-existing Church. Monks with medical or martial training found themselves in great demand during the Crusades, and the battlefields around Jerusalem were littered with the bodies of the injured and dying. Monasteries were pressed into service or willingly offered their skills to serve the pilgrims and Crusaders in need.

Later orders of knights were created for different services: further incursions into the Holy Land and battles against Spain's Moorish border to name a few. While control over the Holy Land ebbed and swelled, the purposes of such military orders became less clear. Knightly groups which form during this period are likely to be more fanatical and more focused towards combat and seizing lands controlled by the enemy. They were trained and ordered to invade, seize keeps and lands, and then hold those territories against the constant assaults of the Muslim enemy.

Later, knightly orders became far less spiritual, and the Church lost a great amount of control over the militant groups. They became orders of advisors, artists, and councilors to the king. With the loss of the Holy Land and the lack of interest in regaining it – along with the weakening of the Catholic Church's hold over secular power – the knightly orders shifted radically in their purposes. There was no longer any need for martial orders to fight against the Muslim threat or reclaim Moorish lands. Therefore, knightly orders foundered and fell, losing significant political hold and finding their lands, status, and monies commandeered by heads of state.

These later groups were only considered knightly orders in a loose sense, taking their prestige from the legends of King Arthur and other chivalric tales. They occasionally had a martial purpose, but if they did it was always in an advisory state. They were no longer soldiers, but instead they were members of a prestigious social class with access to the king's ear.

When creating your order, think about the political situation at hand in your campaign. Is there a dangerous wilderness that travelers must cross to get to a sacred site? If so, a hospitaller order would be right. Is there a threat – particularly one of religious significance – to the land or the people of the faith? If that's the case, you'd want to create a militant order, whose mandate is to wipe out this threat. If neither of these conditions exist, the more social order is probably the right model to use. Keep all of this in mind when creating your new order.

Primary Location

An integral part of creating a knightly order is determining its original location and its primary capital. Some of the most famous orders (the Knights Templar, Knights Hospitaller) were founded in Jerusalem, but their greatest impact was in Spain, Aragon, and other nations outside the Holy Land. The location where the knightly order will function must be considered in order to create a fleshed-out and functional group.

Knightly orders created in Spain or Portugal, near the lines of battle with the Moors, are more likely to be fanatic warriors. They are constantly at war with their enemies, battling over a regularly changing border and against overwhelming odds. These knighthoods are martial in structure, relying on their fierce training and unswerving loyalty to drive back the enemy from the lands of the Christian kings.

Those orders created in England, however, are more prone to be chivalric and less martial. Far away from the battles of the Holy Land or the Moorish border, these knights know little of war. They are focused around serving the Church and protecting the innocent – all of critical importance within the chivalric ideal – rather than spending their time at war. English knights tend to be more courtly and less militant.

The knights of the Holy Land are often more religious and less martial. They are usually hospitallers, tending to pilgrims and defending the city of Jerusalem. They do not usually seek to attack the Moors or Muslims, and were not thrown out of the city when it was retaken. These orders are far less fanatic against the Muslim opposition and primarily focus on helping the needy and keeping the peace.

In Germany and Northern Europe, the Knightly Orders were outstandingly militant – but hardly fanatical in their religious beliefs. Perhaps the least "faithful" of the orders, the German knighthoods were primarily interested in protecting their people and keeping the northern European people pure and safe from southern (Moorish) influences. These knights are perfectly willing to kill and fight, but their zeal comes from patriotism rather than religious fervor.

Purpose

Knightly orders of the Middle Ages can be divided into two primary functions: hospitallers, and soldiers. In the later years of the Middle Ages and into the Renaissance, a third function came into being: the advisors. Almost all knightly orders can be broken down into these three purposes.

Soldiers

The fighting orders are those whose purposes include such sweeping statements as "Kill them all, God will know his own." They are militant groups designed and trained for heavy-duty fighting against infidels, and they are organized very much like a military hierarchy. These orders of knighthood are armies that fight for a specific cause – to rid Spain of heretics, to defend the Holy Land from Muslim interlopers, or to destroy all Moors along the southern borders of the Christian kings. Their purposes are simple, and they have little interest in anything other than dying as martyrs for their cause.

Because the pope is the titular leader of these organizations, they owe little allegiance to king or country. They fight in their own vanguard, using their skills and abilities as they see fit rather than fitting neatly into the armies of the whole. These orders frequently begin as a loose confederation of armed men, guarding pilgrims or fighting to save Christian vanguards on the edge of the Holy Land.

Hospitallers

Hospitaller orders frequently begin as monastic groups, already trained in medicine and healing. They learn fighting as is necessary to protect themselves, their hospices, and to save the injured on the battlefield during fierce combat. These orders rarely dedicate themselves to combat, preferring to tend to religious needs and medicinal issues rather than proving themselves on the field of battle.

Compassion does not necessarily remove the fierceness of these individuals, however. In some cases, hospitaller orders are as warlike as their soldier cousins. They are taught to fight in their own self-defense and on the field of battle when retrieving the wounded and saving lives. They are also taught the essentials of fighting against a siege, so that they can protect their hospices and keeps from invasion.

Advisors

Primarily a function brought into the knightly orders in the latter days of the Middle Ages, the knights who serve as advisors to a king are the least of the orders. These individuals might not be monks; indeed, they might not have any religious fervor at all. Further, they might not even be trained soldiers or in any way capable of wielding a weapon. Their battlefield is that of politics and the royal court; they are advisors to the king, and keepers of state secrets rather than soldiers in a holy war.

Individuals within these brotherhoods are chosen by the king of a nation to be honored with entry into the knightly order. They are typically experienced courtiers with years of service to the throne, and they are dangerous in their own right. The trouble with these orders, of course, is that entry and exit is entirely at the whim of the sovereign, and more than one enterprising courtier was beheaded for "treason" simply because the new monarch did not agree with his induction.

Oaths

All members of Knightly Orders swear oaths upon their induction, regardless of the purpose or goals of the order itself. Historically, most were similar to those sworn by priests upon their confirmation – oaths to the Catholic Church, requesting God's intervention in the knight's life, and promising to live with chastity, humility, and obedience. The knight-to-be made solemn vows to defend the Church, be true to the king, and help women in distress. He repeated the oaths of his order, dedicated himself to its service and the hierarchy of the knighthood. Further, a knight must swear to dedicate his life to right, justice, and holy sanctity.

Knighthoods also possessed their own particular oaths. Some swore allegiance to the pope and his dictates; others vowed never to act against the king or his emissaries. Some promised to eradicate infidels wherever they were found while others swore to protect the needy and help the helpless. The order itself typified and outlined its expectations of its knights, and everyone who swore the oath of the order was expected to live up to the knighthood's standards and protocols.

When you create your own order, think about the oaths that an inductee must swear to become a member. They will be bound up in the order's goals, and they will be taken extremely seriously by all members, most especially the higher ranking ones.

How Do I Join?

Joining a knightly order is easier said than done. First of all, they often have strict standards for entry, and a prospective knight must prove his lineage, background, and faithfulness to the Church. He must also prove that he is a loyal servant of God (or, in the case of secular orders, that he is a citizen of the nation in good standing).

In the Middle Ages, it was not unknown for a knight to be created on the battlefield for his prowess or for some great accomplishment. These knightings (also known as dubbings) were only done by kings, and the inductee often found himself on the short end of their order. Although such members were respected for their prowess and prestige, they were considered lesser knights until they proved themselves to the order as well as to the king.

Later, in the Renaissance, the knightly orders became property of the kings of various countries, and only through his command could a member join. Such orders were designed to be prestigious, and the king nominated and inducted those he felt were worthy of such recognition – often, without even asking the current members.

Because the office of knighthood was treated with so much regard, to be forsworn and stripped of knighthood was a purposefully traumatic experience. The king could make the determination to remove knighthood from a man, as could certain courts. In nearly all instances, the degraded man's spurs were "hacked from his heels," his sword broken (sometimes over his head), his coat of arms burned, and his shield hung upside down in a Church or other public place. Often this disgrace was matched with a death sentence since such knights were often charged with and found guilty of treason.

Mechanics

When designing mechanics for your knightly order, we recommend that you take the following ideas into consideration. Knightly orders are created for a purpose; a cause is given to them from the moment of their founding – occasionally, even before they are granted official recognition. Designing this purpose and setting the campaign around it may be a very interesting backdrop. Creating mechanics for the order should take a back seat to establishing their historical precedent, but mechanics can easily add to the flavor and flair of your new knightly order. Different fraternities of knighthood lend themselves more easily to certain mechanics: warrior-knights can establish prestige classes to give themselves more weapons and abilities to use against their enemies; monastic knights may research new spells or magical blessings to aid their endeavors; advisory bodies often have exceptional courtier skills and spy capabilities. Keep the unique flavor of your knightly order in mind as you create the special mechanics, and this will help add greater flavor and background to your campaign.

All of the orders in this book have two special abilities associated with membership. None are powerful, but they all reflect the general outlook and approach of the orders in question. ***Hospitaller orders do well with bonuses to Heal or perhaps limited use of Cure Light Wounds. The soldier ones get bonuses to hit their hated enemies in combat. Social orders have Skill Bonuses that aid them in court.*** Make it worthwhile to join the order, but don't overdo it.

CREDITS:

Text:
Ree Soesbee

Artwork:
Terry Moore Strickland

Layout:
Christine Whitmer

Art Direction:
Peggy Gordon

Editing:
John R. Phythyon, Jr.

OPEN GAME LICENSE Version 1.0a

The following text is the property of Wizards of the Coast, Inc. and is Copyright 2000 Wizards of the Coast, Inc ("Wizards"). All Rights Reserved.

1. Definitions: (a)"Contributors" means the copyright and/or trademark owners who have contributed Open Game Content; (b)"Derivative Material" means copyrighted material including derivative works and translations (including into other computer languages), potation, modification, correction, addition, extension, upgrade, improvement, compilation, abridgment or other form in which an existing work may be recast, transformed or adapted; (c) "Distribute" means to reproduce, license, rent, lease, sell, broadcast, publicly display, transmit or otherwise distribute; (d)"Open Game Content" means the game mechanic and includes the methods, procedures, processes and routines to the extent such content does not embody the Product Identity and is an enhancement over the prior art and any additional content clearly identified as Open Game Content by the Contributor, and means any work covered by this License, including translations and derivative works under copyright law, but specifically excludes Product Identity. (e) "Product Identity" means product and product line names, logos and identifying marks including trade dress; artifacts; creatures characters; stories, storylines, plots, thematic elements, dialogue, incidents, language, artwork, symbols, designs, depictions, likenesses, formats, poses, concepts, themes and graphic, photographic and other visual or audio representations; names and descriptions of characters, spells, enchantments, personalities, teams, personas, likenesses and special abilities; places, locations, environments, creatures, equipment, magical or supernatural abilities or effects, logos, symbols, or graphic designs; and any other trademark or registered trademark clearly identified as Product identity by the owner of the Product Identity, and which specifically excludes the Open Game Content; (f) "Trademark" means the logos, names, mark, sign, motto, designs that are used by a Contributor to identify itself or its products or the associated products contributed to the Open Game License by the Contributor (g) "Use", "Used" or "Using" means to use, Distribute, copy, edit, format, modify, translate and otherwise create Derivative Material of Open Game Content. (h) "You" or "Your" means the licensee in terms of this agreement.
2. The License: This License applies to any Open Game Content that contains a notice indicating that the Open Game Content may only be Used under and in terms of this License. You must affix such a notice to any Open Game Content that you Use. No terms may be added to or subtracted from this License except as described by the License itself. No other terms or conditions may be applied to any Open Game Content distributed using this License.
3. Offer and Acceptance: By Using the Open Game Content You indicate Your acceptance of the terms of this License.
4. Grant and Consideration: In consideration for agreeing to use this License, the Contributors grant You a perpetual, worldwide, royalty-free, non-exclusive license with the exact terms of this License to Use, the Open Game Content.
5. Representation of Authority to Contribute: If You are contributing original material as Open Game Content, You represent that Your Contributions are Your original creation and/or You have sufficient rights to grant the rights conveyed by this License.
6. Notice of License Copyright: You must update the COPYRIGHT NOTICE portion of this License to include the exact text of the COPYRIGHT NOTICE of any Open Game Content You are copying, modifying or distributing, and You must add the title, the copyright date, and the copyright holder's name to the COPYRIGHT NOTICE of any original Open Game Content you Distribute.
7. Use of Product Identity: You agree not to Use any Product Identity, including as an indication as to compatibility, except as expressly licensed in another, independent Agreement with the owner of each element of that Product Identity. You agree not to indicate compatibility or co-adaptability with any Trademark or Registered Trademark in conjunction with a work containing Open Game Content except as expressly licensed in another, independent Agreement with the owner of such Trademark or Registered Trademark. The use of any Product Identity in Open Game Content does not constitute a challenge to the ownership of that Product Identity. The owner of any Product Identity used in Open Game Content shall retain all rights, title and interest in and to that Product Identity.
8. Identification: If you distribute Open Game Content You must clearly indicate which portions of the work that you are distributing are Open Game Content.
9. Updating the License: Wizards or its designated Agents may publish updated versions of this License. You may use any authorized version of this License to copy, modify and distribute any Open Game Content originally distributed under any version of this License.

10 Copy of this License: You MUST include a copy of this License with every copy of the Open Game Content You Distribute.

11. Use of Contributor Credits: You may not market or advertise the Open Game Content using the name of any Contributor unless You have written permission from the Contributor to do so.

12 Inability to Comply: If it is impossible for You to comply with any of the terms of this License with respect to some or all of the Open Game Content due to statute, judicial order, or governmental regulation then You may not Use any Open Game Material so affected.

13 Termination: This License will terminate automatically if You fail to comply with all terms herein and fail to cure such breach within 30 days of becoming aware of the breach. All sublicenses shall survive the termination of this License.

14 Reformation: If any provision of this License is held to be unenforceable, such provision shall be reformed only to the extent necessary to make it enforceable.

15 COPYRIGHT NOTICE
Open Game License v 1.0 Copyright 2000, Wizards of the Coast, Inc.

Noble Knights © Copyright 2003, Avalanche Press, Ltd.